The Making of a London Suburb

For Lucie

THE MAKING
OF A LONDON SUBURB

Capital comes to Penge

Martin Spence

MERLIN PRESS

First published 2007 by The Merlin Press Ltd.
96 Monnow Street
Monmouth
NP25 3EQ
Wales

www.merlinpress.co.uk

ISBN 9780850365894

British Library Cataloguing in Publication Data
is available from the British Library

Printed in the EU by L.P.P.S. Ltd. NN8 3PJ

Contents

Maps and illustrations   vi

Acknowledgements   vii

Introduction: An ordinary little place   viii

Part I. Context

1. 'The bourgeoisie has created enormous cities':
   Capital and the city   1

2. 'Only magnificent': The growth of London   11

3. 'The suburbs of your good pleasure':
   The growth of South London   27

Part II. The making of Penge

4. 'A wood for fifty hogs of pannage':
   Penge to the eighteenth century   37

5. 'A very valuable parcel of land':
   The enclosure of Penge Common   47

6. 'Speculations of a profitable traffic':
   The Croydon Canal   69

7. 'The crowning work': The railways   77

8. 'Opulent residents with elegant mansions':
   An early Victorian suburb   93

9. 'The wonderful building on the Penge Hills':
   The Crystal Palace   103

10. 'A waste of modern tenements':
    Life in Penge in the late nineteenth century   109

11. Conclusions   119

Bibliography   123

Index   127

Maps and Illustrations

Penge in Context c.1840 map   xi

Key to maps on pages 45, 89 and 99   xii

Penge 1775 map   45

Crooked Billet inn, Penge Common   46

Croydon Canal. View in Penge Wood   68

Penge 1837 map   89

Royal Watermen's and Lightermen's Almshouses,
      Penge, c.1890   90

King William IV Naval Asylum, Penge Lane, Penge   91

North Surrey District School   92

Penge 1851 map   99

Penge 1871 map   99

Crystal Palace site before construction   100

Steam engine used during construction
      of Crystal Palace, 1853   101

Navvies employed in construction of Crystal Palace   102

All illustrations courtesy of Bromley Libraries. The maps are by the author.

Acknowledgements

Thanks to David Cormack, Gary Craig, Lucie Dutton, Roy Lockett and Andrew McCulloch for various forms of help, support and interest. Thanks also to Simon Finch and his colleagues in the Bromley Local Studies Library. And last but certainly not least, thanks to Tony Zurbrugg and Adrian Howe of Merlin Press for their advice, their patience, and their belief that this little book was worth publishing.

Martin Spence

Introduction
An ordinary little place

Penge is an unpretentious, unremarkable, resolutely unfashionable railway suburb, adrift in the low-rise sprawl of south-east London. It is an ordinary little place. But its ordinariness is precisely the point of this book, because the histories of ordinary little places like Penge are packed with interest, drama and insights into the world in which we live.

This is not an exercise in 'local history' as that term is often understood. It is not a miscellany of recollections of bygone days, nor is it a chronicle of colourful local characters, events or anecdotes. It is, instead, a study of the transformation of the local landscape during the key period from the late eighteenth century to the late nineteenth century when Penge was transformed from a semi-rural hamlet into a thoroughly urban railway suburb. Its focus is upon the changing uses to which land was put and the changing ways in which land was exploited as this transformation took place. It argues that this process, the urbanisation of Penge, can only be understood as part and parcel of London's emergence as the first capitalist world-city. In other words, in order to make sense of Penge's development, we must grapple also with the development of London, and the nature of capitalism, and the relationship between capital and cities.

Hence the book's sub-title. It is sub-titled 'Capital Comes to Penge' because it analyses the emergence of this little suburb as part of a wider process of capitalist urban development. It is also a bit of a joke: Penge is one of those place-names that amuse people, somehow lending itself to gentle mock-heroic teasing. But once we've got past the joke, the notion of 'capital coming to Penge' does have a serious message.

In everyday usage, the term 'capital' is often employed quite loosely. Sometimes it is intended simply as a rather pompous synonym for money; sometimes it refers to a fundamental economic resource such as plant or fixed investment ('capital goods'). But the word is not used here in any of these senses. It is used instead it in the much richer, more profound way that Karl Marx used it. It refers to a social process, a *social relation* which obliges people to deal with each other primarily as buyers and sellers in a market – a market furthermore in which the only thing that most people have to sell is their own time, energy and creativity; their own capacity for work; their labour power. So when we talk half-jokingly about 'capital coming to Penge', we are referring to the process whereby this little place was caught up in a social revolution or transformation in which market forces came to dominate all other forms of social relationship, and in doing so created the world – including the built, physical environment – in which we live today.

The book is divided into two parts. Part I sets out a broad theoretical and historical framework as a context for the detailed local story told in Part II. You don't absolutely have to tackle Part I before reading Part II – but it will help if you do, if only because it introduces a few rather specialist terms which appear again later.

Within Part I, Chapter 1 discusses the role of cities in capitalism and capital accumulation; Chapter 2 develops this discussion with reference specifically to London's development from the sixteenth century onwards; and Chapter 3 homes in on South London's place in this process.

In Part II, we look specifically at Penge. Chapter 4 sets the historical background up to the mid-eighteenth century. The following chapters then look in turn at various projects which physically redefined the local landscape. the enclosure of Penge Common (Chapter 5); the Croydon Canal (Chapter 6); the coming of the railways (Chapter 7); population, housing and road-building in the 'early suburb' of the 1830s and 1840s (Chapter 8); and the Crystal Palace (Chapter 9). Chapter 10 presents an overview of life in Penge in the late nineteenth century.

Finally, Chapter 11 draws the threads together to review the various ways in which a study of an ordinary little place like Penge can shed light on London's emergence as the first capitalist world-city, and Britain's emergence as the first industrial capitalist society.

PENGE IN CONTEXT c. 1840

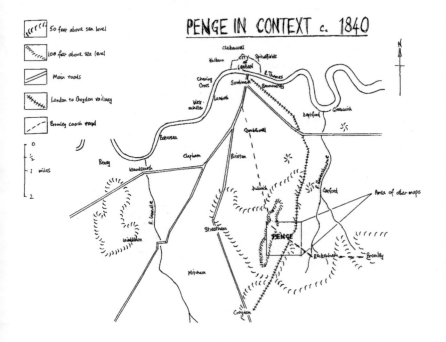

Key:

- 50 feet above sea level
- 100 feet above sea level
- Main roads
- London to Croydon railway
- Bromley coach road

0
½
1   miles
2

N

Clerkenwell
Holborn
Spitalfields
City London
Charing Cross
R. Thames
Southwark
Bermondsey
Westminster
Lambeth
Deptford
Greenwich
Putney
Battersea
Camberwell
Wandsworth
Clapham
Brixton
Dulwich
R. Ravensbourne
R. Cranelle
Cranford
Area of other maps
Wimbledon
Streatham
PENGE
Beckenham
Bromley
Mitcham
Croydon

Common land: wood/pasture

Woods

Farm land/smallholdings

Parkland

Enclosure: undeveloped

Built-up, houses etc.

Trackway

Road

Canal

Railway

PART I

Chapter 1
'The bourgeoisie has created enormous cities': capital and the city

The idea of the city – a permanent, built settlement where people congregate in numbers – is rooted in our sense of history and identity. Cities such as Babylon, Jerusalem, Mecca or Rome are not simply places on the map, but resonant symbols of power, divinity and sin. Our cultural and religious traditions speak of cities as Holy or Celestial, or as a Whore or a Great Wen. Cities move us and excite us, and we use them to represent our own best and worst characteristics.

But once we move beyond myth and symbol, once we try to grapple with cities as material factors in human history, then we have to move beyond thinking of 'the city' in the abstract, as if first century Rome worked in the same way as tenth century Seville or twentieth century London. Of course, all cities share certain fundamental characteristics: they all provide a fixed built environment where a relatively large number of people comes together in a relatively compressed physical space. But beyond this limited definition we must accept that there are many different types of city, growing and evolving in accordance with very different laws of motion.

We are concerned here with one particular type of city: the capitalist city. In order to understand what is special about the capitalist city, it may help to consider its immediate predecessor in Western Europe, the medieval city.

The politics of most major European medieval cities – including London – were dominated by constantly re-negotiated, intrinsically fragile trade-offs between three powers: the crown or state, the Church and the market. The market most certainly existed, and market forces operated, but only within prescribed and jealously guarded limits. All the main social players – including the market's own practitioners: guilds, tradesmen, craftsmen, merchants – acted to keep it in its proper place. Markets were understood to be driven not by abstract 'market forces', but by socially-agreed rules appropriate to their institutional settings.

The capitalist city, by contrast, is a city in which the market is the single dominant force. And precisely because it is the dominant force, and is not forced to share the terrain with other institutions of equal status, it operates in a qualitatively different way from the medieval city with its discreet and constrained zones of market activity. The driving logic of the medieval market was the reproduction – but not necessarily expansion – of its own institutions and social practices. The driving logic of the capitalist market is boundless accumulation, growth feeding on growth.

The close relationship between capitalism and cities has long been recognised. Marx and Engels saw it in 1848:

> The bourgeoisie has subjected the country to the rule of the towns. It has created enormous cities, has greatly increased the urban population as compared to the rural...

But why should this happen? Why should the bourgeoisie, the capitalist ruling class, create enormous cities? What is it about cities which serves the interests of capital?

Capitalism is a social order based on the principle that goods and services are produced not primarily for their intrinsic utility, but rather as commodities to be sold for a profit in a market. This is a very peculiar arrangement. Marx stressed that it does not exist naturally:

> ... Nature does not produce on the one hand owners of money or commodities, and on the other hand men producing nothing but their labour-power. This relationship has no natural basis....

In order to function, this bizarre arrangement requires certain social conditions to be created and actively reproduced, three of which are particularly relevant here:

Firstly, it requires a labour market, where a large number of people (workers) with no other means of livelihood sell their skills and abilities for cash wages to a smaller number of people (employers) willing and able to pay for those skills and abilities. Unlike alternative arrangements such as slavery or serfdom, the mutual obligations on employer and worker are limited to the contract: the employer is not responsible for the worker's family, or health, or housing; and the worker is not bound to a particular master or place. This makes the labour market much more flexible and responsive to capital's unpredictable needs than slavery or serfdom could ever be.

Secondly, it requires a consumer market bringing together a range of cash commodities with consumers willing and able to buy them.

Thirdly, it requires a communications infrastructure for moving people, goods and information from one place to another. People need to move to find work; goods need to move to find buyers; and information needs to move to inform the movements of both people and goods.

Where these conditions exist, capitalist production can occur. And where capitalist production occurs, it grows. It grows not as a means to an end, but as an end in itself. Growth or accumulation is its nature. Capital progresses in the same way as a drunk progresses down a street: the drunk keeps moving forward not because he has any clear idea of where he wants to go, but simply because the fact of motion keeps him upright. So it is with capital. Although it may generate practical, useful goods and services, this is not its primary aim. Its primary aim is simply to grow, and to create the conditions for further growth. This endless accumulation requires investment, and investment requires surpluses of money, raw materials, and – most important of all – surpluses of labour power. And this is where cities come in, because a city is a place where large numbers of people congregate, which makes it a highly convenient place for a surplus of labour power to be accessed and mobilised.

Surplus labour power

The term 'surplus' suggests excess, which is precisely the point. Capital accumulation creates an excess of labour power, a supply of labour power over and above immediate needs. It does this for two reasons.

Firstly, a surplus of labour power can be mobilised at short notice to respond to new or shifting market opportunities. And secondly, the visible presence of workers without work can serve as a standing threat to those in work, reminding them of their vulnerability, reminding them that they can be replaced if they demand better wages or working conditions. Marx called this surplus labour power the 'industrial reserve army' and Mumford summed up the situation in this way:

> It was the manic depressive rhythm of the market ... that made the large urban centre so important to industry. For it was by drawing at need on an underlayer of surplus labour, fitfully employed, that the new capitalists managed to depress wages and meet any sudden demand in production.

The production of space

It was suggested above that the fundamental definition of a city is a relatively large number of people coming together into a fixed built environment within a relatively compressed physical space. No built environment is given by nature. Every built environment, every city, is created by human labour within its own cultural context. In the case of the capitalist city, Lebfebvre suggested that urban space should be analysed in the same way as other products of the market: thus he referred to 'the production of space'. He had twentieth century urban development in mind when he coined this phrase, but it can with equal force be applied to earlier phases of capitalist urban development.

By 'the production of space' we mean the appropriation and restructuring of the urban landscape around the interests of capital: the production of a built environment organised for commodity production, circulation and consumption. This production of capitalist space requires a vast commitment of investment resources in the form of money or credit, raw materials, and labour power.

However, once produced, urban structures become a form of fixed social capital, the value embedded within them effectively frozen or tied up in a fixed physical form. For Marx:

> Fixed capital ... remains within the production process as use value, in a specific material presence.... the value is imprisoned within a specific use value

Harvey has developed this point to argue that the production of capitalist urban space or built environment represents an increase in the organic composition of social capital in a way which is analogous to the increase in the organic composition of capital within an industrial enterprise. In the short-run, in both cases, new investment in fixed capital – machinery in a factory, buildings and urban infrastructure in a city – appears to be rational as it gives the enterprise or city a leading edge. But over time depreciation sets in and the advantage conferred by the fixed capital is lost, and may even become an active hindrance to further accumulation:

> ... we can expect to witness a perpetual struggle in which capitalism builds a physical landscape appropriate to its own condition at a particular moment in time, only to have to destroy it ... at a subsequent point in time.

This means that the production of capitalist urban space highlights in a particularly acute way the tension at the heart of all capitalist production between exchange-value and use-value. Urban infrastructure such as housing or public transport has always experienced cycles of growth and stagnation. In nineteenth century capitalist cities these crises were often highly dramatic, hinged directly to the raw dynamics of accumulation; more recently they have been mediated by public policy and intervention; but instability itself is always present. However even in the most dramatic collapses where bankruptcy wipes exchange-values out of existence, a physical legacy of practical use-values is usually left behind in the form of buildings, roads, railways, sewers, water and gas pipelines, electrical and communication systems, all ready to be snapped up to feed into the next wave of accumulation.

There are, of course, instances where ageing urban structures lose both exchange-value and use-value, and yet linger on despite the fact that the focus of accumulation has shifted elsewhere. Such structures – derelict factories and warehouses, unused roads and paths and railways – slip out of the circuits of capital altogether to become 'wasteland' or – more flatteringly – 'urban countryside'. However even this status is provisional, contingent on capital's changing needs and priorities. Thus industrial riversides in the UK which were entirely derelict 25 years ago have since been re-invented as residential, retail, entertainment and business zones in a carnival of state-sponsored accumulation.

The capitalist city is therefore a particular form of city, whose physical structure and built environment are organised around commodity production, circulation and consumption. The capitalist city is also, by definition, 'modern'. But this should not be taken to mean that it is particularly advanced or sophisticated when judged in human terms or when compared to other forms of city. On the contrary, Mumford provides extensive evidence of the many ways in which capitalist urban space is actively regressive, rejecting sophisticated urban and architectural forms in favour of a narrowly uniform approach, throwing up structures which may be profitable to build and let, but which are crude and dysfunctional as places to live and work. Thus in the early capitalist cities, inhabitants were forced to endure buildings and streets whose foulness, filth, gloom and stink would have been unimaginable in the medieval cities which preceded them. And today we see an enforced uniformity of urban design and architecture, based upon a single energy-intensive model of urban life, which may be highly profitable in the short-term, but which in the medium-term makes the world's cities increasingly indistinguishable from each other; and in the long term is a major source of unsustainable energy consumption and destructive climate change.

Turnover time

Central to capital's endless pursuit of growth is the 'annihilation of space by time', the reduction to a minimum of the time taken to produce a commodity, get it to market, and get it sold. This is the turnover time, and it is crucial to the overall profitability of any capitalist enterprise. For capital, time really is money. Other things being equal, longer turnover time means lower profits.

This means that the city, cramming together large numbers of producers and consumers in a compressed physical space, provides a wonderful opportunity for capital. The city creates the conditions for rapid movement of and dense communication between its people, allowing commodities to be produced, circulated and consumed very quickly, much more quickly than would be possible over a larger territory with a more thinly-scattered population. The production of capitalist urban space is concerned above all with the creation and reproduction of physical structures which exploit and enhance this urban potential for rapid turnover time.

Conclusion

The capitalist city therefore brings together all the ingredients for accumulation. It provides a readily available labour force, and a readily available body of consumers, and it packs them tightly into a physical space with the potential for rapid turnover time, a

potential which is continually enhanced through the production
and reproduction of capitalist urban space.

Capitalist urbanisation is often discussed as if it were essentially
a matter of technological forms, of architectural design or mass
transport systems, but this is not so. Capital's aim, its driving
force, is not technological innovation, but its own growth and
accumulation. New technology may be a convenient means to
this end, but it is only one such means, and it only makes sense
in certain circumstances. There are alternative models of accumulation – for instance, by forcing workers to work long hours
for low pay, or by using human muscle-power to reduce the time
taken to get products to paying customers. The city, which brings
together large numbers of workers and large numbers of customers in a compressed physical space, offers precisely the conditions
for these alternative models. Unskilled or semi-skilled workers
labouring in sweatshops can generate healthy profits so long as
wages are kept low and turnover-time tight. If we are looking for
a classic form of urban capital accumulation, then historically the
low-tech sweatshop has a much stronger claim than the hi-tech
factory.

The city therefore acts as a sort of nursery or hothouse ena-
bling capital to put down roots and flourish. This does not mean
that capital has no interest in the countryside: on the contrary, it
needs the land, raw materials and labour which rural areas provide. Nor does it mean that capital was born in the city and then
expanded outwards: on the contrary, a global network of trad-
ing links was a necessary precondition for the first emergence
of capitalist production in England, Italy, the Netherlands and
elsewhere. Nor does it mean that the capitalist urban dynamic is
a straightforward, seamless story of success: on the contrary, it
has always moved in fits and starts, constantly generating crises,
contradictions, barriers to its own further development.

But even with all these provisos, it remains true that the city
provides capital with a peculiarly supportive environment. It
combines a ready surplus of labour power with a ready body of
consumers, and a physically compressed infrastructure of urban

space allowing for rapid turnover time. Capitalism as a social order aims at chaotic, boundless growth, and the city offers a human and spatial arena which underpins and sustains that chaotic growth.

Sources

Harvey, David, 2001(a). 'The geography of capitalist accumulation' in *Spaces of Capital*, Edinburgh University Press, Edinburgh.

Harvey, David, 2001(b). 'The geopolitics of capitalism' in *Spaces of Capital*, Edinburgh University Press, Edinburgh.

Lefebvre, Henri, 1973. *The Survival of Capitalism*, Allison & Busby, London.

Lefebvre, Henri, 1991. *The Production of Space*, Basil Blackwell, Oxford.

Marx, Karl, 1954. *Capital: A Critique of Political Economy (volume 1)*, Lawrence & Wishart, London.

Marx, Karl, 1973. *Grundrisse*, Penguin, Harmondsworth.

Marx, Karl & Engels, Frederick, 1968. 'Manifesto of the Communist Party' in *Karl Marx and Frederick Engels: Selected Works in One Volume*, Lawrence & Wishart, London.

Mumford, Lewis, 1940. *The Culture of Cities*, Secker & Warburg, London.

Mumford, Lewis, 1961. *The City in History*, Penguin, Harmondsworth.

Chapter 2
'Only magnificent': The growth of London

'London ... is not a pleasant place; it is not agreeable, or cheer-
ful, or easy, or exempt from reproach. It is only magnificent.'
Henry James

Population growth

The relationship between capital and the city sketched in the previous chapter is dramatically illustrated by London's development from the sixteenth century onwards.

In 1550 – a few years before Elizabeth I came to the throne – London's population stood at about 75,000, making it an average-sized European capital city. Over the course of the next century the number of inhabitants exploded, reaching 200,000 in 1600, and 400,000 in 1650. In a single century the city's population had grown by 500 per cent while the population of the rest of England had expanded by only 60 per cent. By 1700 London was home to 575,000 people and was the most populous city in Western Europe: the numbers in its eastern suburbs alone were four times greater than those in Norwich, the second-largest city in the kingdom. In 1750 its population stood at 675,000, representing 10 per cent of the entire population of England and Wales. By 1800 it contained around a million people. Over these 250 years, from 1550 to 1800, its population had grown relentlessly, and at a remarkably steady rate, roughly equivalent to a net increase of ten new inhabitants on every single day.

But the story was far from over. 1800 marked the tipping point at which arithmetical growth turned geometrical. In the first half of the nineteenth Century London's daily growth saw not ten new inhabitants, but 100. And in the second half of the century, each day brought well over 200. The population passed 3 million around 1850 and 7 million around 1900. The world had never seen anything like it.

The point cannot be over-emphasised: London is not just another city. London is unique. No other great capitalist city saw such a record of steady, unbroken growth going back over centuries to the dawn of the capitalist era itself. London is the extraordinary, teeming, filthy, brilliant, shameful exemplar of urban capitalism.

For its first 300 years – from the mid-sixteenth century to the mid-nineteenth century – growth was fuelled by inward migration. Every year London sucked in thousands of people, mostly young people, from the rest of the country. This was only sustainable because London's pattern of life and death, its demographics and mortality, were unique. London was lethal. Over-crowding, poverty, disease and violence – both informal and institutional – kept life expectancy low. Widespread infanticide added to the effect because for many women, such as the thousands of domestic servants, pregnancy was a catastrophe which would cost them their livelihoods. During the eighteenth century infant mortality in some areas rose as high as 74 per cent, and London's death rate regularly exceeded its birth rate. Without immigration London would have become depopulated.

Bubonic plague provides a fair illustration of the unique nature of London's mortality. In the sixteenth and seventeenth centuries plague was endemic in the country as a whole. But when it broke out, as it did in 1563, 1603, 1625 and 1665, its impact was not equally felt. It was infinitely more dreadful in the tightly-packed and infested streets of London than anywhere else. In the last and most notorious outbreak in 1665, 80,000 people died in London – a number equivalent to the combined populations of the country's five largest provincial cities. Even if the effects of plague are discounted, life expectancy in the City of London in the early seventeenth century was still only 25 to 30 years, as compared to 46 years in the countryside.

And yet people – especially young people – kept on coming in from the countryside, and London kept on growing. Its growth was driven by a self-perpetuating cycle of rural push and urban pull.

Key to this cycle was enclosure. Medieval landowners' rights over their estates brought with them a complex bundle of obligations to the rural population. In particular, the rural poor enjoyed customary rights of access, mainly for grazing and fuel-gathering, to areas defined as 'common land'. However, from the sixteenth century the nobility and gentry increasingly took the view that common land was, or ought to be, their private property. They started fencing it off – 'enclosing' it – and denying access to the rural poor.

Enclosure represented the radical renunciation of an entire moral order: in an earlier period it would have been unthinkable. But following Henry VIII's dissolution of the monasteries in the 1530s, it was eminently thinkable. Dissolution is often discussed as if its main significance lay in its religious and diplomatic impacts, or in the personal dilemmas it generated amongst members of the royal family and ruling elite. But dissolution was above all a massive transfer of wealth. It involved the forcible confiscation from the monasteries of millions of acres of prime arable land and pasture, and their acquisition by the Crown and favoured private landowners. At one stroke the independent power and wealth of the Church was broken, and the class structure of the English countryside was transformed, as whole layers of nobles and gentry were enriched with new lands, and through that enrichment bound irrevocably to the Tudor state. Dissolution was an object lesson in licensed lawlessness, as ancient debts of respect and obligation were cancelled by raw state power. If the Church itself could be treated with such contempt, what hope for the traditional rights of small farmers and rural labourers?

Enclosure of common land took different forms, sometimes a simple matter of brute force, on other occasions carrying a veneer of legality. But either way, the practical outcome was the expulsion of a portion of the rural population from land which had supported them and their ancestors for centuries. These people were literally cast out. They faced a brutal choice: starve, throw themselves on the mercy of the parish, or head for a town or city which by virtue of its size offered at least the hope of a new livelihood. And the biggest city, offering the broadest range of hope, was London.

A steady stream of displaced rural workers therefore headed for London from the later sixteenth century onwards and swelled its population, while outside London the population of the country as a whole was hardly growing at all. Sustained growth of the national population only got under way in the late eighteenth century. For 200 years, therefore, London was effectively depopulating the countryside. In the half century from 1650 to 1700, for instance, London's population grew by 175,000 while the population of the rest of England fell.

Once in London, people who had previously been agricultural producers became urban consumers. London acquired a new and hungry population at the same time, and for the same reasons, as the countryside was losing its workforce. The only way to square the circle was for agriculture to adapt: firstly by moving away from local or regional subsistence and towards a market-based focus on meeting the city's needs; and secondly by pushing up overall productivity.

This agricultural transformation went through different phases. In the sixteenth century production in London's immediate agricultural hinterland switched away from arable farming, and towards livestock and hay production, to meet the city's needs. But by the end of the eighteenth century a Middlesex farmer described the areas closest to London as entirely given over to market gardens. What was true of Middlesex was also true of Hertfordshire and Essex, and – to a somewhat lesser degree because of poorer roads and access – of Kent and Surrey. Farms across much of south-east England were overwhelmingly focused on feeding the city.

Rural change was therefore inseparable from urban growth, yoked to it in a cycle of transformation which fed upon itself.

Enclosure pushed the rural poor off the land and into the city, which changed them from net producers of food into net consumers, which forced farmers to increase productivity and focus on cash-crops for the city, which reinforced the rationale for a cash-driven capitalist approach to farming and land-ownership, which led to further enclosure.

A similar self-reinforcing dynamic can be seen at work in London itself, because its sheer size meant that it acted as a powerful population magnet.

London's economic base was very broad. The single largest source of paid employment was in cloth, and especially the finishing trades: dress-makers, milliners, tailors, weavers and others made up perhaps 20 to 25 per cent of all jobs in the late eighteenth century. Next in importance were the ports, docks and shipyards: it is almost forgotten that London was the country's main ship-building centre from the late sixteenth to the mid nineteenth century. Shops, public houses, retail and catering employed about 12 to 13 per cent of the workforce. Then came food and drink manufacture (e.g. breweries and distilleries); transport; the building industry; domestic service (accounting for 6 to 7 per cent of all workers in the eighteenth and nineteenth centuries); leather goods; and metal work and engineering.

For those lucky enough to have a job, London paid relatively well. There was a definite London wage premium, a differential between London wages and those in the rest of the country. This differential was wider in some periods than others: it was substantial in the early sixteenth century; fell back in the later sixteenth and early seventeenth centuries; widened in the second half of the seventeenth early eighteenth centuries; narrowed from about 1750; increased again in the 1820s, and so on. But it was always there.

No displaced rural worker believed that the streets of London were paved with gold, and many would have realised that the odds were stacked heavily against finding a steady job and a secure income. But the sheer size of the place, the range of its economic activity, meant that it offered options, it offered hope, which was not available elsewhere. Of those who came seeking their fortunes, some succeeded in making a decent life for themselves, but many failed. In the seventeenth and eighteenth centuries, about one quarter of the entire population was made up of beggars or casual workers.

Meanwhile, for those higher in the social scale, London was a magnet for rather different reasons. From the sixteenth century, in many European countries, the royal court settled itself more or less permanently in its capital city, and this happened in England too: the centralised despotic Tudor state was very much a London-based state. This created a host of opportunities for courtiers and hangers-on, and jobs for administrators and clerks to staff the growing governmental bureaucracy. These in turn created consumer markets for refined food and drink, fashionable clothing, and household furniture and accessories, which pulled in tradesmen and craftsmen from far afield. John Stowe lamented in the late sixteenth century that London's prosperous, fashionable classes were actively impoverishing the rest of the country by monopolising its supply of skilled labour.

This convergence of economic activity and political power meant that much of the country's personal wealth was concentrated in the hands of families which lived, permanently or seasonally, in and around London. The flotation of the Bank of England in 1694 provides a neat illustration: 87 per cent of its subscribers, providing 90 per cent of its capital, lived in London, Middlesex, Surrey or Hertfordshire.

The production of suburban space

London's explosion in population, and in the value and volume of urban economic activity from the sixteenth century onwards, was associated with an explosion in the volume of urban space in the suburbs. These were more than just overspill from the overcrowded City. They had their own rationale. They were actively and deliberately exploited by new entrepreneurs as sites for new forms of capital accumulation which directly challenged the vested interests of the City.

'Suburb' means an area outside or beyond (sub) the city (urb). London's early suburbs were of course geographically outside the City walls. But more significantly, they were outside or beyond the regulatory reach and authority of the guilds, corporations and other institutions of the City of London whose roots lay in the medieval past. The suburbs were zones of unlicensed entrepreneurial activity, unlicensed production and circulation, where new markets were created to exploit the naked imperatives of supply and demand, rather than the carefully orchestrated mixed economy of market forces, social obligation and protectionism championed by the guilds.

The guilds could see what was happening and they tried to resist the trend. They petitioned Crown and Parliament repeatedly from the late sixteenth to the early seventeenth centuries. They obtained various proclamations and Acts which sought to stop or restrict further suburban expansion – but it went on regardless. Suburban entrepreneurs were establishing the principle of the market as the single prime mover of city life and urban growth, and no pious declaration would stand in their way.

It is no surprise, therefore, to find that Adam Smith, the foremost champion of the unfettered free market, positively advocated making use of the suburbs precisely because they fell outside the influence of the guilds. He objected strongly to the guilds' grip on employment practices and opportunities. He even objected to their charitable role on behalf of the poor, sick, widows and orphans, which in his eyes diverted resources which would be better employed in profitable investment. Instead, Smith urged:

> If you would have your work tolerably executed, it must be done in the suburbs where the workmen, having no exclusive privilege, have nothing but their character to depend upon ....

His advice was widely followed, notably in the various clothing finishing trades which were so important to London's economy. Thus immigrant French hatters were settled in Battersea and Wandsworth in the late seventeenth century, and provided a ready-made workforce for skinners and merchants who wished to avoid the corporate jurisdiction of the feltmakers. And the Company of Weavers was fatally undermined by the appearance of non-guild silk weavers in the north-east suburbs.

The same trend can also be seen in wholesale and retail activities. The meat trade provides a good example, occupying as it did a central place in the wider system of food supply to the city.

Traditionally there were four licensed meat markets at Smithfield, Stocks, Newgate and Leadenhall. These were linked to the ancient guilds and companies of the trade. But as the city expanded and its population grew, its appetite for meat became gargantuan: by the mid eighteenth century, 74,000 sheep were being sold at Smithfield every day. The sheer scale of activity and market opportunity made it increasingly difficult for the traditional markets to defend their old privileges.

Instead, new unregulated markets appeared beyond their jurisdiction in the suburbs, dominated by ruthless commercial dealers. These new men operated outside the boundaries of the old moral economy: their business was driven by cash. One result was that bad and adulterated produce regularly found its way to consumers, contributing to the generally poor health of the city's inhabitants.

London's growing appetite for meat also provided another link in the chain which bound urban growth to rural transformation. The need to move thousands of animals to market each day provided a very immediate and practical motivation for road-building and turnpikes. Once built, these new roads were a whole new factor in the rural landscape. They made it easier and quicker to get all sorts of agricultural goods to paying customers, and so encouraged more and more farmers to increase their productivity and to focus on the crops and livestock which London wanted to buy.

London's suburbs were therefore active agents in its expansion. They were not simply the passive recipients of growth spilling over from the City: they were motors of growth, much of which took the form of a direct challenge to the City and its institutions.

The suburbs of the seventeenth century included neighbourhoods such as the Strand to the west of the City, where nobles and churchmen had their town-houses from medieval times; Covent Garden and the new 'West End', fashionable by virtue of its proximity to the court; Grays Inn, Holborn and Clerkenwell, convenient areas from which lawyers and clerks could operate; Spitalfields, Whitechapel and Wapping to the east, magnets for the poor and the embryonic proletariat; and across the river there was Southwark, where a great church and bishop's palace sat cheek by jowl with brothels, theatres and bear-baiting dens. Taken together, by 1700, these and other suburbs accommodated 80 per cent of London's population, leaving only 20 per cent living in the City itself.

This physical expansion in the volume of urban space created new opportunities for landowners and landlords, and nurtured a new attitude towards land and buildings. Notions of stewardship were replaced by a new focus on exploitable cash value, on the maximum rental income which could be generated from a given plot. And this in turn encouraged a tendency to treat land as an abstract investment opportunity without regard for historic usage or social obligation.

This was a tendency, not an absolute rule. And it encountered real barriers – not least from the fact that a lot of land in and around London was governed by ancient long-term leases based on feudal rights and medieval notions of land-use. Even so, an energetic commercial landlord in the seventeenth and eighteenth centuries would find plenty of scope for profit.

First and foremost, such a landlord was a pragmatist. He was certainly not committed to the erection of new buildings for their own sake. On the contrary an existing building, which might date back far into the city's medieval past, would be highly prized so long as it could still generate a rental income, for instance by serving as a slum tenement. Housing the poor was highly profitable. They were a constant and reliable presence: as we have seen, there was a steady flood of inward migration for three solid centuries from the mid sixteenth century onwards. Being poor, they could not pay a sufficient rent to justify building new houses. But if they could be crammed sufficiently tightly into already-existing tenements or cottages or basements or attics, then they were a profitable proposition. The rent per head was low, but the rent per square foot was more than could be achieved in any other way. Overcrowded slum housing was therefore the normal living arrangement not just for beggars and the destitute, but for a large slice of the low-paid working class as well.

Where new houses were built, they were intended primarily for tenants higher in the social scale who could pay a sufficiently high rent to justify the cost of building. Even so, the same short-term pragmatism is evident here as in the approach to housing the poor. The difference is that here, it expressed itself in the materials used, and in the design and layout of the new houses.

In the sixteenth and early seventeenth centuries, most new building simply replaced previous structures within the framework of the medieval street plan. At the end of the sixteenth century, John Stow observed that the favoured approach of commercial landlords was to replace old stone buildings of perhaps two storeys, by new wooden-framed buildings with four or five storeys. This combination of different building material and more floor space effectively increased the financial returns from a given plot.

It also raises an intriguing question about the Great Fire of 1666. The Fire only took hold because of the quantity of wooden-framed houses in the City and suburbs immediately to the west. Standard accounts of the Fire routinely blame these houses for its rapid spread, and routinely refer to them as 'medieval'. But Stow's observation implies a more complex picture. Stow observed medieval stone buildings being deliberately demolished to make way for wooden-framed buildings, purely for reasons of profit. There is no reason why this trend should not have continued for a further 70 years between Stow's time and the Fire, so it may be that blame for the destruction done by the Fire should rest not with ancient wooden buildings inherited from the medieval city, but rather with new wooden buildings put up by profit-seeking commercial landlords from the late sixteenth century onwards.

When it came to design, market pressures encouraged a process of abstract standardisation. As ever, the aim was to maximise the rental income from a given plot, but because new-build housing was intended for tenants higher in the social scale, this had to be balanced against considerations of style and fashion.

London landowners' solution in both City and suburbs in the seventeenth and eighteenth centuries was the terrace. The terrace might present a carefully crafted face to the street, with doors and windows tastefully and proportionately designed, but nevertheless it was essentially a means of cramming many separate households onto a given plot. Each individual house took the form of an oblong with a narrow front and considerable depth, so that a large part of the interior space had little or no access to natural light or air. Mumford described such degraded upper-class dwellings as 'intolerable super slums'.

The commercial and contractual motor driving forward this production of suburban space was the 'building-lease system'. Some form of this had been in place since the sixteenth century, but it was brought to a pitch of ruthless perfection by Dr. Nicholas Barbon or Barbones after the Great Fire. Barbon had a particular talent for spotting opportunities for profit in post-Fire London: not only did he perfect the building-lease system, but he also pioneered fire insurance and organised the city's first fire brigade.

In the building-lease system, the landowner leased his land to a builder for a fixed number of years. The builder put up a number of houses on the land – sometimes closely supervised by the landowner, sometimes not – and was then at liberty to rent the houses out to tenants for the period of the lease. By now, of course, the builder might be deep in debt, firstly because of the cost of the lease, and secondly because of the costs of construction. If he could find paying tenants quickly and get his money back, all well and good. If he failed, and was unable to meet his obligations under the lease, then the land reverted to the landowner

– together with a brand new set of houses that the landowner had effectively acquired for free.

This system drove forward the mass production of capitalist suburban space by providing positive incentives to both land-owner and builder to develop as much land as possible, as quick-ly as possible, on an entirely commercial profit-making basis. Although modified over the years – the length of a long-term lease rose from about 40 years in the mid seventeenth century to 99 years in the eighteenth century – the building-lease system was still being used in all its essentials in the early twentieth cen-tury. The brutal brilliance at its heart was that even if the chain of financial and legal obligations snapped, even if the builder went bankrupt, still it guaranteed the production of a concrete use-value in the form of a group or terrace of houses where none had stood before.

London and British capitalism

London's population growth took off in the sixteenth century, driven by a massive and sustained flood of immigrants from the countryside who came in search of a livelihood. This created a large and continuing surplus of labour power. In addition, by virtue of its size, and its status as a major port and trade centre, and as the seat of monarchy and government, London generated consumer demand for a vast range of goods and services. And its physical compression, the compact density of its urban space, allowed for rapid turnover time, with people and goods mov-ing around quickly and in bulk. London brought together the key pre-conditions for urban capital accumulation with a venge-ance.

Conventional economic analysis today distinguishes 'manu-facturing' from 'services', with the implication that manufactur-ing activity will be technology-based and capital-intensive, while service activities will be relatively labour-intensive. But these conventional notions fail to capture the character of the economy of London in the eighteenth and nineteenth centuries where both services and manufacturing were highly labour-intensive.

It is often forgotten that throughout the capitalist era London has been a major manufacturing city. Throughout the eighteenth and nineteenth centuries it was in fact the country's greatest manufacturing city, dwarfing Birmingham or Manchester in terms of output and employment. One reason why this is forgotten is that, despite its size, London's manufacturing sector is easily lost in the shadow of the even larger service sector. And a second reason is that with certain exceptions such as brewing, London manufacturing was not in general at the cutting edge of technological innovation or engineering technique. Much London manufacturing was labour-intensive, sometimes employing skilled artisans, but more often relying on unskilled labour through sweatshops and home-working. The enormous cloth industry is the prime example. It made its profits through the imposition of long hours and low pay, backed up by the disciplinary presence of the unemployed, which itself was constantly-renewed by the steady flow of immigrants – a vast industrial reserve army ready to take the places of those currently in work.

The same labour-intensive logic operated in other major areas of the city's economy attributed conventionally to the service sector: its shops; public houses and hotels; the building industry; domestic service; transport; and trade, which encompassed both the mass manual labour of the ports and docks, and the mass clerical labour of the City with its banks, insurers, shipping companies and legal firms.

None of this makes London unusual: we saw in Chapter 1 that the sweatshop has a stronger claim to be regarded as the classic form of urban capital accumulation than does the highly-mechanised factory. And the demand generated by low-tech, labour-intensive, sweatshop labour can act as a stimulus to technological innovation elsewhere. Thus it was with London in the eighteenth century: by virtue of its sheer size, bulk, and the frenzied pace of its economic activity, London acted as a catalyst for the generalisation of capitalist production throughout the country. Its enormous demand for food, together with its steady depopulation of the countryside, stimulated a revolution in agricultural technology and land-management aimed at increasing productivity per acre. And its demand for a whole range of manufactured goods – including raw material to feed the sweatshops of its own cloth finishing-trades – prompted the construction of the country's first truly mechanised factories, with spinning and weaving machines powered by the fast-running rivers of the Pennines.

All of this calls into question the conventional assumption that the driving force behind the development of capitalism in Britain was the 'Industrial Revolution' of the late eighteenth and early nineteenth centuries. It is easy to understand why this idea is appealing. It is simple to grasp. It is satisfyingly hard-headed and pragmatic. It privileges issues of technology, invention and engineering accomplishment. And it sits easily with the view that machines and technological traditions are somehow neutral, mere embodiments of engineering technique to be used for good or ill, regardless of the social or historical context in which they arise.

This vision is familiar and appealing, but it is false. The technological innovations of the Industrial Revolution did not make possible the rise of capitalism in Britain. On the contrary, they were pragmatic responses to market opportunities opened up by already-existing capitalist social relations, above all in the feverish, over-crowded hot-house of London. Once established, of course, the new technologies gave a further impetus, a new dynamic, to the overall process of accumulation. But the essential point stands: technological innovation is an option for capital, but it does not define it. Other models of accumulation – raw exploitation, sweatshops, long hours, low pay – are not only available, but tend to be favoured where cities act as nurseries of capital, as London did from the sixteenth to the nineteenth centuries.

Sources

Harwood, Elain & Saint, Andrew, 1991. *London*. HMSO, London.

Hobsbawm, E.J., 1968, *Industry and Empire*, Weidenfeld & Nicholson, London.

Inwood, Stephen, 1998, *A History of London*, Macmillan, London.

Jones, Edward & Woodward, Christopher. 1992. *A Guide to the Architecture of London*. Weidenfeld & Nicholson, London.

Linebaugh, Peter, 1993. *The London Hanged*, Penguin, Harmondsworth.

Miele, Chris, 1999. 'From aristocratic ideal to middle class idyll: 1690-1840' in *London Suburbs*, Saint, Andrew (intro.), Merrell Holberton, London.

Mumford, Lewis, 1940. *The Culture of Cities*, Secker & Warburg, London.

Mumford, Lewis, 1961. *The City in History*, Penguin, Harmondsworth.

Porter, Roy. 1996. *London, a Social History*. Penguin, Harmondsworth.

Schofield, John. 1993. *The Building of London from the Conquest to the Great Fire*. Sutton Publishing, Stroud.

Sheppard, Francis, 1998. *London: A History*, Oxford University Press, Oxford.

Thorold, Peter. 2001. *The London Rich*. Penguin, Harmondsworth.

Chapter 3
'The suburbs of your good pleasure':
The growth of South London

The idea of the suburb

To our ears, the word 'suburb' carries a number of cross-cutting meanings and associations: pleasant, alienating, cosy, boring, neighbourly, philistine, or any combination of these. But underlying them all is an unspoken assumption that a suburb is primarily a place to live: a residential suburb. This was not always true: as we have seen, London's suburbs from the sixteenth century were not only places to live but also, crucially, zones of unlicensed, unregulated, or disreputable economic activity.

Consequently, in Shakespeare for instance, the word carries rich and damning implications which may be lost to our twenty-first century ears. In *Julius Caesar*, Portia seeks to shame her husband Brutus by asking him:

> … Dwell I but in the suburbs
> Of your good pleasure? If it be no more,
> Portia is Brutus' harlot, not his wife.

Shakespeare's contemporary Thomas Nashe made the same point even more directly:

> London, what are thy suburbs but licensed stews?

This easy, natural association of suburbs with dishonourable and illicit trade, and specifically with prostitution, made perfectly good sense to Shakespeare's audience. The reference would have carried added piquancy if the lines themselves were delivered at the Globe Theatre in the heart of Southwark, which, with its brothels, taverns and bear-baiting, was the most disreputable of all London's suburbs.

The meaning of the term has therefore shifted and changed over time from a place of ill repute to a place which may be otherwise respectable but where unregulated or unlicensed economic activity takes place; to a place offering a quiet, semi-rural, relatively privileged residential retreat from the city. From an early date, South London offered embryonic forms of all these suburban types.

South London in the mid eighteenth century

At the start of the eighteenth century South London – which was then mostly the northern wedge of Surrey – consisted of two very different zones.

Firstly, along the south bank of the Thames immediately opposite the City, and along the River Wandle, South London was as industrialised as anywhere in the country. There were shipyards from Southwark to Deptford; Bermondsey had leather works, tan yards and glue factories; and Lambeth was famous for its potteries. A mile or two to the west, the Wandle was a thoroughly industrial river. Its steep fall from Croydon and Carshalton had for centuries been used to generate water power for mills: the Domesday Book lists thirteen corn mills along its length as early as the eleventh century. It fell comfortably outside the influence of the guilds and companies of the City of London, and by the eighteenth century it boasted mills and factories dealing in corn, copper, iron, oil, leather, paper, snuff, gunpowder, and textile printing.

The Southwark/Deptford riverside and the Wandle represented industrial South London. But further back from the Thames, east of Deptford, and west of Wandsworth, the area had a very different character. Since the Middle Ages, it had been favoured by royalty, nobility, and clerics as a rural retreat which was conveniently situated for easy contact with the City and the Court.

The Archbishops of Canterbury had a palace in Croydon from about the twelfth century; royal palaces were built at Nonsuch, Kennington, Greenwich and Eltham; and aristocrats and gentry established houses in the area, including the Heydons at Wickham Court in the fifteenth century, and the Carews at Beddington Place some years later.

South London, therefore, had a long tradition as a place of rest and recuperation for the elite, and from the seventeenth century this role expanded to offer a broader social appeal. The key to this new development was the discovery of spas. The healthy properties of natural spring water were already well-known: merchants took the waters at Epsom, and aristocrats did likewise at Tunbridge Wells. In the mid seventeenth century spas were discovered at Sydenham in 1641, and at Streatham in 1659, and these quickly became popular places for day-trips. Unlike Epsom and Tunbridge Wells, according to Daniel Defoe, these attracted the 'common people'. In fact the spa at Sydenham attracted such a large gathering in 1651 that it alarmed the Commonwealth Government which sent in the cavalry.

Meanwhile, the population of the City and its immediate suburbs continued to grow: by 1650 it had been growing steadily for a century. We have already seen what this meant for the poverty-stricken majority of its people, crammed ever more tightly into the city's slums. Eventually, inevitably, a trend set in whereby those who could afford it started to move away so as to escape the endless squalor, the stench of streets and rivers which served as open sewers, and the physical danger of living among a vast population of the unemployed with no means of livelihood and little to lose by resorting to robbery or worse.

The Fire of 1666 was a pivotal moment in this trend: many who were forced to find lodging away from the City during the rebuilding never came back. But it didn't start with the fire: as early as 1613 Edward Alleyn, impresario and brothel-keeper, decided to make himself respectable by buying the Manor of Dulwich. In a similar spirit, a few decades later, Samuel Pepys retired to Clapham after a long career as civil servant, diarist and philanderer. Merchants, businessmen and civil servants were following in the footsteps of the courtiers and prelates and starting to carve out their private retreats among the woods and hills of South London. And as they did so, a different sort of suburb started to take shape: suburbs in the new, aspirational, residential meaning of the word. Created by middle-class flight, each new neighbourhood sought to project itself as discreet, safe, respectable and physically distant from the dangers and the stink of the bloated city.

South London's suburbs

As the seventeenth century gave way to the eighteenth, certain parts of South London established themselves as desirable residential areas for the new, fast-growing middle class. Clapham had a regular coach service into the City from 1690 and started to acquire fashionable terraces, just like parts of central London, a few years later. Camberwell Grove was also well regarded. And further out, a few energetic businessmen settled in Epsom and commuted every day into the City by horse.

These new residential suburbs were at pains to distinguish and distance themselves from the city but they were, of course, utterly dependent upon it. They acted as privileged retreats from some of the more obnoxious aspects of city life, but in order to pay for these retreats, their residents needed daily access to that city. Easy communication across the Thames – bridges – were therefore vital if South London's new suburbs were ever to grow beyond a light scattering of villas and terraces in a few selected hamlets and townships.

In 1700 London Bridge was still the only fixed crossing. Throughout the seventeenth century there had been plans to build new bridges across the river, each of which had run up against opposition from the City, and specifically from groups such as the Watermen and Lightermens Guild whose members earned their living by ferrying passengers across the Thames. They successfully scuppered plans for bridges at Westminster in the 1660s, and Putney in the 1670s.

However the watermen were not the only vested interest involved. Landowners south of the river were acutely aware that the value of their estates was only a fraction of the value of equivalent land just a few hundred yards away on the opposite bank. As the eighteenth century progressed, large blocks of land in South London came into the hands of a few powerful aristocratic magnates, including Earl Spencer and the Duke of Bedford. These men had formidable political connections which they were more than willing to exploit in order to raise the value of their landholdings. In 1738 Westminster Bridge became the second fixed crossing across the river, followed by Blackfriars Bridge in 1769 and Battersea in 1771. Battersea Bridge in particular illustrates the importance of powerful aristocratic players with a commercial interest in South London's suburban development. Its main backer on the south bank was Earl Spencer, whose family acquired the Manor of Battersea in the 1760s. He quickly set about creating the conditions for the transformation of his new land into middle-class residential suburbs. A riot of building took off from the 1770s. Its target market was the aspirational middle class, but its main instigators and beneficiaries were aristocratic landowners eager for profit.

Within this orgy of building, a social pecking-order of size and style was established. Neo-classical villas set in parkland served the wealthiest (Plaistow Lodge; Addington Palace); the gentry commissioned substantial houses in more modest grounds (Beckenham Place; Belair; Norwood Grove); and the upper middle class settled for fashionable terraces or, from the early nineteenth century, detached and semi-detached houses arranged in groups or estates.

In the early years of the nineteenth century South London's new respectable upper-middle-class suburbs included Brixton, Denmark Hill and Herne Hill. Wealthy Jewish, Huguenot, Portuguese, and French financiers and businessmen favoured South London in growing numbers. This was noted by William Cobbett in 1823; his writing reflects both seething contempt for money-men and casual anti-Semitism:

> Between Sutton and the Wen [i.e. London] there is, in fact,
> little besides houses, gardens, grass plats and other matters
> to accommodate the Jews and jobbers and the mistresses
> and bastards that are put out a-keeping.

By 1829, there were 100 different coach services linking the City
to Clapham, Brixton, Dulwich and Blackheath.

And yet, as the nineteenth century progressed, and the building went on, it became increasingly difficult for these suburbs to
retain their character as exclusive retreats reserved for the prosperous middle class. Three factors contributed to this: the middle
class way of life itself; the railways; and the building-lease system.

The demands of social status and respectability required any
family with pretensions to middle-class status to employ domestic
servants. In larger and wealthier families, whole teams of servants
lodged permanently in the houses of their masters and mistresses.
And even quite modest lower-middle-class families might have a
house-maid come in each day to clean and to prepare food. In
addition to domestic servants, small armies of tradesmen, craftsmen and suppliers were required to provide food and household
goods, to maintain the fabric of the house, and to tend to the garden. Given that cheap public transport aimed at ordinary workers
simply did not exist, these armies of domestic servants, suppliers,
tradesmen and craftsmen had necessarily to live locally.

As a result, the nineteenth century 'exclusive middle class suburb' carried at its heart a profound contradiction. It promised
a lifestyle of peaceful domestic leisure, far from the dirt, smells,
dangers and social complexity of the city, in a community inhabited exclusively by other impeccably respectable neighbours. And
yet this peaceful middle-class leisure was underpinned by an
enormous volume of intensive manual labour, performed within
the family house itself or in the immediate vicinity by people who
were, by definition, workers. The exclusive middle-class suburb
necessarily called into existence its own local working-class population. And over time this working-class population necessarily

acquired its own local identity, and generated its own demand for shops, pubs, schools and chapels, and gave a new socially-complex and expansive character to the area, far from the narrow middle-class respectability intended by its original builders and residents.

The second factor which could undermine the exclusive social character of these suburbs was the railway. The relationship between London's railways and its suburbs is complex, and depends very much on local factors and on timing. Thus Penge is a text-book railway suburb, in that the arrival of the railway was a necessary precondition for its early development as an upper-middle-class residential area.

However, where a respectable suburb had already established itself prior to the coming of the railway, its arrival could have precisely the opposite effect. Clapham provides a good illustration. Clapham established itself as a genteel residential area in the seventeenth century, and retained this character for 200 years. In the early nineteenth century it was the home of the 'Clapham Sect', a group of wealthy and godly businessmen who preached a message of sobriety and piety to the country's ruling class, with sufficient success to be credited with having 'created Victorianism'. It was also the home of Thomas Cubitt, the doyen of suburban builders, who set out to create at Clapham Park the archetypal middle-class estate. As late as the 1850s there were plans to re-launch Clapham as a southerly extension of the West End, 'another Belgravia', by means of a new road bridge across the Thames.

And yet within a few years, despite this long tradition of middle-class respectability, and despite its powerful local champions, Clapham was defeated by the railway. Its dreams of linking up with the West End were shattered when two powerful railway companies, the London Chatham and Dover Railway Company (LCDR), and the London Brighton and South Coast Railway Company (LBSCR), purchased a great swathe of land at Battersea and Nine Elms and transformed it into an urban wilderness of railway lines, crossings, sidings, viaducts, and workshops, all centred on an enormous new station called Clapham Junction. This in turn triggered the construction of a mass of houses aimed at a new incoming lower-middle- and working-class population. Pious, respectable Clapham never recovered.

Established working-class communities closer to the river also found themselves under attack from the railways, and here the impact was infinitely more brutal. The simplest way for the railway companies to create space for their new lines was to demolish thousands of homes. And yet all too often the residents had nowhere else to go: their families, and job opportunities, were still close by. So they just crammed themselves even more tightly into the remaining space. In the name of peace and fresh air in the new outer suburbs, the railways thus created misery and overcrowding in older suburbs close to the Thames.

Finally, the exclusive social character of South London's new suburbs was progressively undermined by the economics of the building lease system.

We have already seen how the building lease system operated, harnessing the inherent anarchy of the market so as to maximise the volume of buildings erected. It achieved this effect through a careful apportionment of risk between landowner and builder. And the way in which this balance of risk worked in practice was a reflection of the highly-fragmented structure of London's construction industry. The building trade was dominated by a large number of small, chronically under-capitalised builders: in 1851 the city had over 700 building companies, of which over 90 per cent employed fewer than 50 workers. When one of these small builders got a new contract, he did not have the luxury of waiting until a suitable number of tenants came onto the market before putting up bespoke houses to order. In order to maximise his chance of a profit he had to try to minimise his turnover time. The temptation was therefore to put the houses up as quickly as possible, and to build them in a style likely to attract prosperous tenants so as to increase his chance of a high rent. Meanwhile, all around, his rivals were doing exactly the same. As long as landowners kept on making their land available, small builders had little choice but to keep on building and hoping for the best.

The result was a classic series of crises of over-accumulation. The industry boomed from 1817 to 1825; slumped from 1826 to 1832; recovered in the late 1830s; boomed in 1846-7; slumped in the late 1840s and early 1850s, and so on. Each boom saw a building frenzy leading to a glut and a crash, with new houses standing empty for months or even years on end – and the longer a house stood empty, the more likely the neighbourhood would lose its allure as newer and greener suburbs opened up further out. Builders regularly went bankrupt, and landowners cut their losses by carving up the spacious but empty family houses on their plots of land for multi-occupation, aiming now at tenants lower on the social scale. Over time many formerly prestigious residential areas slipped downmarket.

The building-lease system was a brutal manifestation of capitalism at its most chaotic. It regularly drove building companies into bankruptcy and condemned thousands of workers to lifetimes of insecurity and recurrent poverty. But as a means of producing capitalist urban space on a large scale it succeeded magnificently. It created a material legacy in the form of hundreds of streetfuls of houses in which we still live today. Much of the London landscape, much of the enduring stock of fixed capital which makes up today's built environment, was created by the building lease system in the nineteenth century.

For all these reasons, suburbs which initially took shape as semi-rural, prestigious retreats for the well-to-do middle class tended, over time, to expand into larger and broader-based communities with a more complex class character. And each time this happened, landowners and builders would get together to put up more houses somewhere new, a few miles further out, and make the same promises of exclusivity all over again.

Sources

Bailey, Paul, 1996, *The Oxford Book of London*, Oxford University Press, Oxford.

Cherry, Bridget & Pevsner, Nicolaus, Pevsner, 1983, *London 2: South*, Penguin, Harmondsworth.

Croydon Natural History & Scientific Society (CNHSS), 1979. *Victorian Croydon Illustrated*, CNHSS Ltd., Croydon.

Cobbett, William, 1967. *Rural Rides*, Penguin, Harmondsworth.

Gilbert, Bob. 1991. *The Green London Way*. Lawrence & Wishart, London.

Inwood, Stephen, 1998, *A History of London*, Macmillan, London.

Jones, Edward & Woodward, Christopher. 1992. *A Guide to the Architecture of London*. Weidenfeld & Nicholson, London.

Miele, Chris, 1999. 'From aristocratic ideal to middle class idyll: 1690-1840' in *London Suburbs*, Saint, Andrew (intro.), Merrell Holberton, London.

Piper, Alan, 1996. *A History of Brixton*. The Brixton Society, London.

Porter, Roy. 1996. *London, a Social History*. Penguin, Harmondsworth.

Sheppard, Francis, 1998. *London: A History*, Oxford University Press, Oxford.

Thorold, Peter. 2001. *The London Rich*. Penguin, Harmondsworth.

Wandle Group, The. 1997. *The Wandle Guide*, London Borough of Sutton Leisure Services, Sutton.

Part II

Chapter 4

'A wood for fifty hogs of pannage': Penge to the eighteenth century

Much of southern Britain after the last Ice Age, about 10,000 years ago, was heavily wooded. This was not the light woodland familiar to us today. The post-glacial woods were wildwood, pristine and daunting. The dominant tree was small-leaved lime – Rackham refers to lowland England at this time as the Lime Province – together with hazel, sessile oak, elm, hornbeam, beech and maple. Beneath the trees were shrubs – holly, hazel and hawthorn – and the land supported a rich range of wildlife including beavers, elk, boar, wild horses and the wild ox.

The first serious organised effort to clear the wildwood came in the Neolithic or New Stone Age. From about 6,500 years ago, and for centuries to follow, the trees were hacked back in order to make land available for agriculture and pasture. By the time of the Iron Age around 500 BC, half of the English wildwood had gone. However, in the Penge area, and along the ridge which later became known as the Great North Wood, the trees survived. This was no accident: Neolithic and Iron Age farmers usually ignored trees on high ground or poor soil because they knew that the effort involved in cutting them down would be disproportionate to the benefit achieved.

We have no direct evidence of local settlement during the Roman, post-Roman or early Anglo-Saxon periods. Penge only formally enters documented history in the tenth and eleventh centuries when charters referred to it first as 'Paenge' and then as 'Penceat'. This is a Celtic/British place-name, and it is intriguing to find that it was still being used at a time when this part of the country was culturally Germanic or Anglo-Saxon.

In the tenth century the nearest Celtic/British kingdoms were far away in Wales and Cornwall. And yet place-names with Celtic/ British references are scattered across South London. 'Camberwell' comes from the word by which the British called themselves, and is related to the modern term *Cymru*, which is the Welsh name for Wales. And 'Walworth' comes from *Wealh*, the Saxon term for the British, which later transmuted into 'Welsh'. The survival of these names suggests that British communities may have lived on locally well into what we now call 'Anglo-Saxon times'. The pattern of Germanic settlement in London left plenty of room for this to happen: the settlers tended to favour rivers and riversides with their easily cultivated soils. Wherever possible they avoided more heavily wooded clay soil such as that found at Penge. So maybe an understanding developed whereby Germanic settlers left the place in the hands of the local British, so long as the local British kept themselves to themselves.

Today, the Celtic/British language survives as Welsh, Gaelic and Breton. 'Paenge' or 'Penceat' might be rendered in modern Welsh as 'Pen y coed' meaning 'Head of the wood' or 'Edge of the wood'. In other words, back in the tenth century, this was a place known primarily for its woods and trees. This is hardly surprising. This whole part of South London was known for its woodland, as many English place-names also testify: names ending in -ley (Bromley, Shirley, Langley) indicate an inhabited clearing surrounded by woodland; names ending in -hurst (Selhurst, Croham Hurst) may indicate the same, or the presence of a wooded hill; and names such as Norwood or Forest Hill are self-explanatory.

The first document to mention Penge was a charter drawn up in 957 in which King Eadwig gave a grant of land to Lyfing, one of his advisers. The charter stated:

> Hereto belongeth the wood that is called Paenge, 7 miles and 7 furlongs and 7 feet round about.

and it described 'Paenge' as belonging to the Hundred of East Brixton and the Parish of Battersea. Eadwig himself was an ineffective king who was soon replaced by his brother, but he was nevertheless fortunate to reign at a relatively stable time. It didn't last: with the eleventh century the country entered a century of turmoil. England was for a while absorbed into Canute's Danish empire; went through a brief period of civil war; lived with a sustained political and cultural tussle between the pro-Norman Edward the Confessor and much of the English nobility; and was finally overwhelmed by the catastrophe at Hastings in 1066 and its brutal aftermath as the Normans imposed their rule.

We look back now at the Battle of Hastings with a thousand years of hindsight. We know too well how significant it was, how much of a break with the past. But at the time, even after their victory on 14th October, the Norman invaders were isolated in a large and hostile country, far from secure. William had to keep the advantage, and he had to satisfy his own followers' lust for land and loot. He adopted a strategy of terror, piling on the pressure, battering the shell-shocked English into despair and submission. He swept through Sussex, Surrey and Hertfordshire, laying waste as he went. When he reached the Thames he made a particular example of the Manor of Battersea, which covered much of South London. He did so for a very specific, very personal reason: Battersea had previously belonged to Harold Godwinson, King Harold, William's recently-defeated foe at Hastings. Most of the Manor was carved up between William's two half-brothers: Bishop Odo got Peckham, while Robert, Count of Mortain, received Streatham and Tooting.

The remaining fragment of the dismembered Manor of Battersea was granted to Westminster Abbey, an act of politically-astute piety on the part of the Conqueror, who went to great pains to legitimise his rule by associating it with the reign of the Abbey's founder, Edward the Confessor. And along with this award went Penge, which was associated with the main body of Battersea despite being several miles away. This was no accident. It was a deliberate act. William's Charter referred explicitly to 'all the chase of the wood Penceat which belongs to the aforesaid Batricseie'.

It may seem strange to us that a scrap of woodland should be linked to a manor or estate from which it was physically cut off, but it was in fact a perfectly normal medieval arrangement. After centuries of tree-felling from the Neolithic onwards, wood was a scarce resource. Many landowners went to great pains to acquire rights over physically distant patches of woodland. Much of the Weald consisted of parcels of woodland belonging to distant set-tlements which needed access to timber, firewood, charcoal, or grazing for their pigs. Penge was no different: it was allocated to Westminster Abbey as a woodland resource, and as such it became a 'detached hamlet of Battersea', a status which it would retain for the next 800 years.

Twenty years after Hastings, William ordered the great stock-take known as the Domesday Book. Although Penge is not named, it is almost certainly the 'wood for fifty hogs of pannage' recorded as belonging to the Manor of Battersea. This means that it con-tained a wood sufficient for fifty pigs to fatten on acorns in the autumn before being slaughtered. Rackham describes pannage as a 'famous but not very important use of wood pasture' but never-theless it tells us two important things about Penge. Firstly, it tells us that the local woods must have contained English oak; and secondly, that by the late eleventh century the woods already had a long history as a carefully managed economic resource.

How do we know this? Firstly, the local oak trees must have included pedunculate or English oak, because this is the species which yields acorns. But despite its name, English oak is not the original native oak tree. The ancient, native oak of post-glacial Britain is sessile oak. Where English oak establishes itself in a zone previously dominated by sessile oak, this generally means that it has been deliberately planted by humans precisely in order to yield acorns to feed pigs. In other words, if Penge's woods contained enough English oak to feed pigs by the late eleventh century, they must have been subject to a long history of care-ful management and controlled planting for many years before that, going back well into Anglo-Saxon times, and maybe even further.

Politically and culturally, the Normans represented a massive and bloody rupture in English history. Economically however, there is a clear continuity from Edward the Confessor's reign in the mid eleventh century through to the mid fourteenth century. This was a period of growth, expansion, population increase, and land hunger. For three centuries more and more land was put under the plough by hacking back the increasingly beleaguered remaining patches of woodland. By the mid fourteenth century, only 10 per cent of the country was wooded. This process was brought up short in the most terrible way: in 1349 the Black Death arrived, cutting down between one-third and one-quarter of the entire population. The clearances stopped. Labour, not land, was now the scarce resource.

Throughout this period Penge remained part of the Manor of Battersea, and Battersea remained part of the lands of Westminster Abbey. This came to an end in the sixteenth century, when the Abbey fell victim to Henry VIII's dissolution of the monasteries. Its lands, like those of hundreds of other religious establishments, were seized by the Crown.

In 1605, just after Elizabeth I's death, a survey was carried out which defined the boundaries of Penge hamlet. We have to guess at the precise location of some of the features described, but a few key landmarks are clearly identifiable today. To the north, the 'common of Rockhills' was close to where the TV transmission tower now stands. In the south-east 'Willmoores Bridge' is the point where Beckenham Road crosses the River Chaffinch or Willmore, a few yards south-east of Clock House Station: this was the traditional county boundary between Surrey and Kent, Penge being in Surrey. The south-west boundary was marked by Croydon Common, roughly where Selhurst is today. And the 'Vicker's Oak' – which used to stand close by the site of the roundabout at the junction of Crystal Palace Parade, Anerley Hill, Church Road and Westow Hill – marked the north-west corner.

The Vicar's Oak stood for about 400 years from the early fifteenth century, and was one of a number of significant oak tree sites in London which acted as important boundary markers, many of which are still remembered in place-names: Honor Oak, Burnt Oak, Gospel Oak, Royal Oak. The special significance of Vicar's Oak was that, perhaps uniquely, it marked the meeting point of four parishes: Lambeth, Battersea, Camberwell and Croydon. Today the four parishes have been replaced by four London Boroughs – Lambeth, Southwark, Croydon and Bromley – but they still meet at exactly the same point.

As a significant boundary marker, Vicar's Oak was a key point of reference in the medieval ceremony of 'beating the bounds'. Carried out every year, this was a part-religious, part-secular event intended both to bless the crops and to mark and re-affirm important communal boundaries including, significantly, the boundaries of the common land. The ceremony was banned in Henry VIII's time on the grounds that it had become 'disorderly' – although we may suspect that the real aim was to discourage an activity which celebrated the institution of common land and thus posed a symbolic challenge to the quasi-official policy of enclosure and privatisation.

After the Dissolution, the Manor of Battersea was passed around within the royal family and aristocracy. Elizabeth I gave it to a favourite called Royden, and by the early seventeenth century it was held by James I's consort, Anne of Denmark. She passed it to her son the Prince of Wales, the future Charles I. He in turn gave it to a favourite called St. John, whose family held it until the second half of the eighteenth century, by which time they had acquired the title of Viscount Bolingbroke.

Meanwhile, Penge's detached relationship with Battersea was causing a problem. Sunday Church attendance was more or less compulsory at this time, and as parishioners of Battersea the residents of Penge were, strictly speaking, expected to make a long round trip every week to Battersea Parish Church. In practice, most went just down the road to Beckenham. This arrangement was eventually formalised by a regular payment from Battersea

Parish to Beckenham Parish for religious services rendered. This payment in turn gives us an early head-count of the Penge population: in 1725 the Vicar of Battersea reported that the hamlet consisted of 13 houses and 50 inhabitants, and he paid a sum based on these figures to his opposite number at Beckenham.

Penge in the middle years of the eighteenth century was therefore a detached hamlet of Battersea, as it had been since the Conquest. The Lord of the Manor was Viscount Bolingbroke. The population numbered about 50. The soil was poor, though it supported a couple of farms: Barnard's Farm and Swingate Farm. The area's main economic resource was its woodland, a fair portion of which had by this time been transformed into wood-heath – land whose trees had been felled so that it could be used for grazing. Both the woods and the wood-heath were common land, used by the residents as a source of firewood, and as pasture for pigs and other livestock.

This all sounds very quiet and rural, but we must not make the mistake of thinking that we are dealing here with an isolated country backwater. Penge lay less than ten miles due south of London, the largest city in Christendom. Since 1715 a stage-coach service from Beckenham had rattled regularly through the hamlet on its way to the City of London, and around 1750 a further service was laid on from Bromley. And Penge's woodlands tied it into the wider economy, providing charcoal for London's bakers, tannin for the leather industry at Bermondsey, and timber for the shipyards at Deptford.

This was the starting point for the making of Penge. Over the next century its landscape was remodelled, and its character transformed. This process was driven by four projects: the enclosure of the Common; the Croydon Canal; the railways; and the Crystal Palace. Together, they provided the catalyst for a tidal-wave of road- and house-building which took off in the 1840s and continued for the rest of the century. Together, they provided the framework for Penge's transformation into a railway suburb of the world's greatest capitalist city.

Sources

Brooke, Christopher, 1967. *The Saxon and Norman Kings.* Fontana, London.

Cowie, Robert with Harding, Charlotte, 2000, 'Saxon settlement and economy from the Dark Ages to Domesday' in *The Archaeology of Greater London,* Museum of London, London.

Croydon Natural History & Scientific Society (CNHSS), 1979. *Victorian Croydon Illustrated,* CNHSS Ltd., Croydon.

Fowler H.W. and Fowler F.G. (eds.), 1964. *The Concise Oxford Dictionary of Current English.* Oxford University Press, Oxford.

Friends of the Great North Wood, 1986, *The Great North Wood*

Friends of the Great North Wood, 1995, *From the Nun's Head to the Screaming Alice.*

Mabey, Richard. 1998. *Flora Britannica* (concise edition). Chatto & Windus, London.

Morris, John. 1973. *The Age of Arthur.* Weidenfeld & Nicholson, London.

Pullen, Doris E. 1971. *Penge,* Able Publications, Knebworth.

Rackham, Oliver. 1986. *The History of the Countryside.* Phoenix Press, London.

Taylor, Bessie. 1965. *Bromley, Beckenham & Penge, Kent, since 1750.* Department of Geography, Birkbeck College, London.

Taylor, John George. 1925. *Our Lady of Batersey.* George White, London.

Victoria Histories of the Counties of England: Surrey, 1967. Reprint of 1912 edition. Dawson, London.

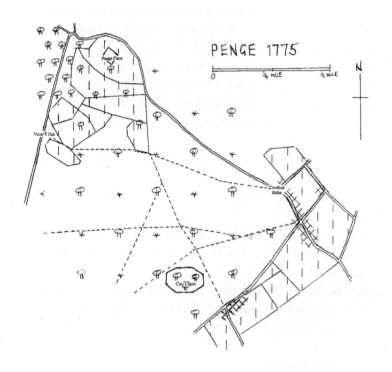

PENGE 1775

0   ¼ MILE   ½ MILE

N

Penge Place

Vicar's Oak

Crooked
Billet

Clay Copse

Crooked Billet inn, Penge Common

Chapter 5
'A very valuable parcel of land':
The enclosure of Penge Common

Introduction

Penge in the mid eighteenth century was a small agricultural hamlet, historically attached to the manor and parish of Battersea. Most of its tiny population lived from the land, probably earning a bit of cash by working on local farms, combined with their own produce from smallholdings, plus access to the resources of Penge Common.

Common rights were long-established customary entitlements, taking different forms depending on local conditions. 'Common of pasture' is self explanatory; 'common of piscary' referred to the right to fish; 'common of turbary' to the right to cut turf for fuel; and 'common of estovers' to the right to gather wood. In the case of Penge, parishioners used the Common to gather firewood, and to graze pigs and other livestock. This didn't mean that they 'owned' it: these rights were not about private property, but were instead rooted in traditional concepts of shared access and benefit. And they were under attack.

Since the sixteenth century landowners had been uprooting customary rights and redefining common land as their own private property by means of enclosure. By the second half of the eighteenth century enclosure was accomplished by getting parliamentary approval in the form of an Enclosure Act. This was generally not difficult. Members of the House of Commons were drawn from the gentry and professions, and were voted in by a tiny electorate also drawn from the gentry and professions. And the House of Lords, enormously powerful and closely linked to the Court, gave political clout to both hereditary and upstart aristocrats. Since the gentry and the aristocracy were precisely the classes which benefited from enclosure of common land, in most cases Enclosure Bills sailed through Parliament without challenge. The whole enterprise was backed up by an ideology of agricultural 'improvement' which regarded common land as synonymous with waste.

The period from the 1750s to the 1780s saw a particularly high level of activity. In those decades, Parliament passed scores of Enclosure Acts which taken together accounted for one-quarter of the country's arable land. When a proposal to enclose Penge Common came forward in the 1760s, therefore, we might expect that it would have attracted little comment and that it would have won easy approval in Parliament. But we would be wrong.

The Spencers

At the start of the 1760s the Manor of Battersea, together with its detached hamlet at Penge, was held by the St. John family, Viscounts Bolingbroke. They had owned it for over a century. They were Tories, but in 1763 they sold Battersea to Earl Spencer, one of the rising stars of the Whig oligarchy which dominated British politics.

The Spencers were well-connected, leaders of fashion, enormously acquisitive, and deep in debt. Earl John Spencer was notoriously profligate, and lived in a style which he felt his title demanded, but which was far beyond his financial means. He bought the Manor of Battersea for its extensive lands close to the river, and it was a good investment: this area was ripe with development potential. Penge simply came as part of the package, and was of no interest to him. So in 1772, in order to raise some cash, Spencer decided to offload the recently-built mansion at Penge Place, together with its estate of 135 acres. It was auctioned off at Christies to John Morgan, a local landowner. However the income from occasional sales such as this was quite insufficient to solve Spencer's financial problems, and by the time he died in 1783 he had brought the family close to ruin.

John Spencer was succeeded as Earl by his son George. George was quite unlike his reckless father. Always religiously devout, in his youth he also flirted with political radicalism. As Earl his views shifted to the patriotic mainstream, and he deserted the Whigs for the Tories. Nevertheless, he was still driven by a strong sense of religious and moral duty which pushed him into public service. Pitt made him First Lord of the Admiralty, in which post he served throughout the Napoleonic Wars, probably playing a role in talent-spotting Horatio Nelson.

Spencer was therefore an influential and well-respected public figure. As a member of the Government and of the House of Lords, he was a formidable force in Parliament. And as Lord of the Manor of Battersea and a devout Christian, he took a close interest in the affairs of the parish. It follows that he was in a powerful position to influence any Enclosure Bill affecting common land in Battersea or Penge, and he made good use of this power. Specifically, at certain key moments, he opposed enclosure in the name of the rights of the parish. This made him highly unusual, almost a contradiction in terms. At a time when Parliament was almost synonymous with the interests of landowners as advocates of enclosure, here was a powerful landowner and Parliamentarian who actually opposed it.

The Battersea Vestry

Local government in eighteenth and early nineteenth century London differed radically from place to place. In the City, there was a system of ward administration going back to the Middle Ages. But most of London now lay outside the City walls, and had seen two centuries of runaway growth without any coherent attempt to set up a system even for such basic functions as maintaining the roads or keeping public order. The result was that responsibility for these tasks fell by default onto the only already-existing institution with local roots, local legitimacy and defined local boundaries: the parish. The governing body of the parish, the parish council or Vestry, was thus the de facto local government.

In Battersea as in many other places, the members of the Vestry were local worthies, tradesmen, householders and small land-owners. Their authority ultimately stemmed from the Church, and a major part of their role was to uphold religious and moral orthodoxy in the local community, to enforce regular church attendance, and to look after the parish Church itself including repairs and re-building. But they also dealt with many secular matters: they administered the Poor Law by collecting an annual rate from residents for the 'relief of the poor'. They appointed overseers to administer poor relief, constables to keep public order, and surveyors to maintain the local roads. And finally, the Vestry was also the guardian of the parish's time-honoured rights in its various patches of common land.

There was nothing unusual about the Battersea Vestry. It went about its work, held meetings, kept minutes, received reports, levied rates and distributed the proceeds, and appointed offic-ers – including special nominees to look after the roads and the poor in its detached hamlet at Penge. In all its dealings it had to take account of the interests and views of Earl Spencer, who as the parish's key patron provided the vicar with his housing and income. But it would be wrong to see Battersea Vestry in the later eighteenth and early nineteenth century as merely a rub-ber-stamp for the Lord of the Manor: during this period, vestries generally enjoyed a fair degree of independence.

John Morgan

In January 1786, the minutes of the Battersea Vestry record that a paper had been fixed to the church door 'supposed to be placed there by the direction of Mr. Morgan Esq. of Penge', giving notice of his intent 'as owner of the Manor of Penge' to present an Enclosure Bill to Parliament.

The Battersea Vestry was not opposed to enclosure as a matter of principle. Its records show that it approved a steady stream of small-scale enclosure proposals on Battersea Common right through the late eighteenth century and into the early nineteenth century. However, in these cases it received suitably respectful petitions, as well as offers of financial compensation for the loss of its corporate rights. By contrast in the case of Penge, Morgan made no petition, and sought to enclose the whole Common at one fell swoop. This was not the way to win the Vestry's support.

In October 1786, after a fruitless meeting with Morgan, the Vestry formally declared its rights on Penge Common and its intention to oppose Morgan's Bill. Two months later it levied an additional rate, partly for the poor but also for 'discharging the expense that may arise from the resolution above relative to Penge'. In today's language, the Vestry set up a fighting fund. Battle was joined with Morgan, and it went on for eight years, including two periods – 1787-8 and 1793-4 – when things became extremely heated.

In May 1787 a Vestry delegation visited Penge and found that some land on the Common had already been illegally enclosed 'by some person or other, particularly a part adjoining the house of Mr. Morgan'. The Vestry members broke down sections of offending fencing erected by Morgan, and by his neighbours messrs. Swabey and Wilson, so as to restore free access to the common land. Swabey and Wilson offered to make payments to the parish in return for keeping their fences, but these offers were rejected and the fences came down.

In the following year the Vestry wrote to Morgan formally instructing him to remove his illegal enclosure on Penge Common. He retaliated by bringing a legal case for damages or trespass against John Harrison, one of the parish overseers, presumably for his role in the fence-breaking episode. The court supported Morgan and fined Harrison. We might expect that respectable members of a parish council would have been horrified to find themselves thus placed on the wrong side of the law, but far from it. They promptly reimbursed Harrison's fine from Vestry funds.

Morgan upped the ante again five years later, when he threatened to prosecute any parishioner turning cattle onto the Common. The Vestry responded by indemnifying all parishioners against

Morgan's threats, and by collecting evidence to back up its own claims. This led to a programme of research and interviews in the early months of 1794 in the course of which old parish records were studied, witnesses were called, and the Vestry's solicitor, Mr. Humphreys of Tooley Street, drew up a summary statement of the parish's rights.

By the time Morgan carried out his threat and took a parishioner to court – Thomas Bartlett, a Churchwarden – the Vestry had its arguments finely honed. They met with Morgan's solicitor and offered him a deal: they would admit to trespass if he would produce title deeds showing that the land was his property, and provide counter-evidence to their witness statements attesting to customary rights on the Common. Not surprisingly Morgan's lawyer refused.

Between these two episodes of direct action and litigation, there was a brief period when it seemed that the whole matter might be settled by throwing money at it. In 1790 a Committee was appointed by the Vestry 'to treat with Mr. Morgan' and in July they reported that he was prepared to pay £200 in respect of the parish's rights on the Common as and when he could muster sufficient Parliamentary support to push through an Enclosure Bill. The Vestry decided to adopt a twin-track strategy. It would continue to oppose Morgan in Parliament, but agreed that if it should lose, it would take the money. Interestingly, at the meeting that adopted this position, each member present was required to put his signature to the resolution in the minutes. This was obviously seen as a controversial decision, on which it was necessary to maintain collective responsibility. In fact it never became necessary to contemplate taking Morgan's money, because time and again his Enclosure Bills were rejected in Parliament, thanks to the efforts of Earl Spencer and his ally Lord Thurlow.

A tantalising footnote. From 1795 to 1797, the Vestry minutes record that 'John Morgan' was elected and re-elected as overseer of the poor for Penge – that is to say, the parish official responsible for administering local poor relief. This must be the same John Morgan, and the Vestry's initiative in making him a parish official – and his acceptance of the appointment – presumably marks some sort of truce between them.

In 1801, Morgan sold the manor of Penge to John Scott.

John Scott

John Scott was Lord of the Manor of Penge for the next 12 years, and at first he showed no sign of any particular interest in the status of the Common. However, other forces were at work which would have a major influence upon its future.

In the early years of the new century the Croydon Canal Company was busily building a new canal from Rotherhithe to Croydon (see Chapter 6). This was sanctioned by Parliament, which effectively gave the Company compulsory purchase powers over its intended route. In 1802 the Company arrived at Penge Common, invoked its powers, acquired nine acres of the Common – and thereby gave a whole new commercial rationale to the notion of enclosure.

Previously the argument for enclosing the Common rested on a broad assertion that in terms of agricultural productivity, private ownership of land was inherently 'efficient' while common land was inherently 'wasteful'. Heath or wood-heath, produced when tree-felling is followed by grazing, was regarded as an especially wasteful form of common land . And Penge Common was classic wood-heathland, with gorse, bracken, bramble and heather under a scattered tree-cover of silver birch, beech, sweet chestnut and oak. However, with the advent of the Canal the prospects of this alleged wasteland were transformed. The broad-brush aim of 'agricultural improvement' was replaced by a much tighter focus on a specific cash-crop – timber – which could now be transported in bulk to a specific market – London. Before the Canal, the job of felling, stripping and hauling timber to London over notoriously bad roads had been desperately slow. Now the turnover time was drastically reduced. It was possible to deliver the goods to the city's ravenous building industry quickly, regularly and promptly.

Despite this potential for new tension, for the first few years of Scott's ownership there was no sign of conflict with the Vestry. In fact Scott was appointed by the Vestry as Penge's surveyor of highways and overseer of the poor. By drawing him into their own circle and making him one of their own, Vestry members presumably hoped to thwart any ambitions he may have to challenge its traditional rights on the Common. It was a continuation of the policy that they had in the end adopted towards Morgan, and for a while it seems to have worked.

However, by 1807 this consensual mood seems to have evaporated. In August of that year Battersea Vestry asked its solicitor to get counsel's opinion respecting 'the rights of enclosures' at Penge. Meanwhile, in July and October, Vestry members gathered at the Crooked Billet to mark out the boundary between its land in Penge and the neighbouring parishes of Croydon, Beckenham (or 'Beckingham') and Sydenham. Boundary posts were put down and their locations recorded with precision in the Vestry minutes:

> One Boundrie post down at Blind Mans Corner, three fields from west gate adjoining Croydon Parish about 300 yards… at the County gate adjoining Beckingham... in the Lane from the sign of the Crooked Billet leading to Sydenham'; '... at Rockers Hill about 40 yards from the Bound Post on Morgan Hill … at Gravil Hill near Thieves Den … about 150 yards from Gravil Hill … at Quains Gap near the Canal … at the White Post adjoining Croydon Parish … at the top of Clay Lane adjoining Beckingham Parish ….

There is nothing in the Vestry minutes to indicate any disputes with neighbouring parishes, so it is unlikely that this solemn procedure of tramping around the boundary was aimed at them. It makes more sense to see it as a collective assertion of traditional rights, common rights, aimed at local landowners within the boundary who had designs on the Common. The most substantial such landowner was Scott, and he seems to have got the mes-

sage. The next formal attempt at enclosure did not come until
1812, by which time Scott was negotiating the sale of his manor
to the Cator family.

The Cators' first bill

John Cator was a successful City businessman, a timber merchant, who had decided to establish himself as a country gentle-
man in the Penge and Beckenham area. In 1773 he bought the
Manor of Beckenham from the St. Johns – the same old Tory
family which had sold Battersea and Penge to the Spencers. The
Beckenham Manor included several farms whose names are still
familiar today: Copers Cope Farm, Foxgrove Farm, and Kent
House Farm.

By the end of the decade Cator had established himself as a
leading member of local society. He built Beckenham Place, a
compact sub-classical mansion set in parkland: today it is the
club-house of a municipal golf course. He ingratiated himself
with the well-connected Norman family in Bromley, and helped
set up the Prince's Plain Cricket Club, membership of which
quickly became essential for aspiring local gentry. And he made
fashionable inroads into the world of art and literature: his guest
list at Beckenham Place included Dr. Johnson, Mrs Thrale, Fanny
Burney and Joshua Reynolds.

Cator must have been aware of the vendetta between his neighbour John Morgan and the Battersea Vestry in the enclosure bat-
tles of the 1780s and 1790s. But for many years he took no interest in the future of Penge Common. Instead he went on extend-
ing and developing his own property. In 1793 he negotiated a
local land-swap with Lord Gwydir, and in the following year he
purchased the newly-built Crooked Billet coaching inn on Penge
Green, which was on the site now occupied by the Watermens
Almshouses.

The first sign that Cator was becoming interested in enclosure
came in 1796, when he was one of several sponsors of a Bill presented to Parliament for the enclosure of Croydon Common. He
followed this up the next year with another Enclosure Bill, this

time aimed at Penge Common. In effect he was picking up where Morgan had left off – Morgan by this time made his peace with the Battersea Vestry. Cator's motives are unclear: maybe he was frustrated by Morgan's surrender, and offended by the survival of a tract of 'wasteful' and unsightly common land so close to his own neat farms and parklands in Beckenham. Whatever his motives, he provoked an immediate and passionate response. As soon as his Bill appeared, Earl Spencer took the lead in opposing it. He wrote to the Vestry to confirm his opposition, worked with it to organise a successful counter petition, and defeated the Bill in Parliament. There is no sign of Spencer taking quite so pro-active a role in any of Morgan's earlier enclosure attempts, which raises a question as to whether he had some particular reason – some personal reason perhaps – to put such effort into frustrating John Cator. It is a question which was to re-surface almost 30 years later.

In 1806 John Cator died, and his estate passed to his nephew John Barwell Cator, son of his brother Joseph.

Scott's Bill

As we have seen, the Vestry undertook a series of defensive manoeuvres in 1807, which for a while dissuaded Scott as owner of Penge Place from making any moves towards enclosure. But this success was relatively brief, and by 1812 Scott's attitude had hardened.

In that year, Scott appears to have accepted a payment from the Croydon Canal Company. The Vestry suspected that this payment was in respect of the nine acres of Penge Common which the Canal Company had acquired in 1802. This outraged them because to accept such a payment clearly implied that Scott regarded himself as the owner of those acres of common land. The Vestry's suspicion was heightened when, in the same year, Scott submitted an Enclosure Bill to Parliament.

This sparked the usual flurry of activity. The Vestry convened a special meeting early in 1813, and set up a Committee to investigate how 'the intended enclosure of Penge Common will affect the rights of this Parish'. It also re-engaged Mr. Humphreys of Tooley Street as its solicitor.

Back in 1790 Morgan had offered £200 to buy out the parish's rights on the Common, and the Vestry had adopted a pragmatic twin-track response: carry on fighting the enclosure, but be prepared to take the money if the fight was lost. Now Scott also made a financial offer, this time of £600. This seems to have been too much to resist: the Committee recommended to the Vestry that this sum be accepted, and the Vestry agreed, so long as the Bill was withdrawn.

This was a much weaker position than the twin-track policy of 1790. Rather than fight and only take the money if it was defeated, the Vestry this time chose a financial settlement as its preferred option. And yet ironically, now that it was willing to surrender, no-one else was listening. Having made his financial offer, Scott appears to have lost interest and concentrated instead on negotiating the sale of Penge Place to the Cator family. In 1813 he sold it to John Cator's brother, Joseph. The following year saw an intra-family transfer whereby Joseph passed Penge on to his son John Barwell, who already held the Manor of Beckenham: the two neighbouring estates of Penge and Beckenham were now in the hands of a single owner. But despite his powerful position, John Barwell Cator did not follow up either on Scott's financial offer or on his Enclosure Bill. For a few more years, Penge Common survived.

The Cators' second Bill

In the years from 1813 to 1826 the Battersea Vestry reasserted its proprietorial interest in Penge, and organised 'perambulations' to assert its traditional rights in 1817 and 1824. Meanwhile, things were not standing still in the wider world. Other enclosures were under way, and the traditional appearance of the countryside of much of south-east England was changing as farms turned to cash-crops and market-gardening to feed London. All of this attracted bad-tempered comment from William Cobbett when he rode through the area in 1823:

When you get to Beckenham, which is the last parish in Kent,
the country begins to assume a cockney-like appearance; all
is artificial and you no longer feel any interest in it.

The final chapter in the saga of the Penge Enclosure opened in
1826, when John Barwell Cator presented a Bill to Parliament for
the enclosure of the Common.

Once more the members of the Vestry geared up for battle, and
their records on this occasion – the occasion of their ultimate
defeat – are more meticulous than ever. As on previous occasions, they set up a special Committee. As on previous occasions,
they appointed a solicitor, this time a Mr. Edge. And as on previous occasions, they prepared their arguments.

In January and February 1827 Edge presented lengthy reports
to the Vestry, setting out its options as he saw them. He con-
firmed the historical and legal basis for the parish's rights on
Penge Common, though he also advised that these rights – such
as the gathering of fuel – had not been actively exercised for a
considerable time. He felt that this would pose a problem. More
significantly, Edge argued that the only people entitled to benefit
personally from the parish's rights were freeholders and copy-
holders. This was a reversal of the traditional view. Traditionally,
it was held that that poor parishioners without property should
be the key group to benefit from rights of commonage, but Edge
proposed that, on the contrary, only property owners should
benefit. It is not clear why he took this view. Maybe he was a
pragmatist who thought that a traditionalist defence would fail,
whereas a property-based defence might succeed. Or perhaps he
was ideologically persuaded of the primacy of individual property rights.

Either way, he was not a defeatist. He advocated an active campaign to defend the parish's rights as he saw them. John Scott
was approached, as former Lord of the Manor of Penge, and was
asked to reveal whether or not he had received money from the
Croydon Canal Company in or around 1812 in respect of the
common land acquired by the Company in 1802. Presumably the

intention was to get Scott to deny having received such a payment, which would also imply recognition – by a former Lord of the Manor, no less – that the land in question was common land and not his to sell.

Much more significantly, the Vestry also resolved to put formal questions to Earl Spencer and to its own Vicar, the Vicar of Battersea 'to ascertain if any and what arrangements have been entered into by them with Mr. Cator respecting the proposed enclosure of Penge Common'.

It is astonishing that the Vestry felt able to address its own Vicar, and its long-term aristocratic patron and ally, in such impertinent terms. Relations had clearly become strained, even hostile, as demonstrated by Spencer's reply, in which he curtly refused to assist the Vestry in any way. And yet for years Spencer and the Vestry had worked together to protect the integrity of Penge Common. What had changed?

The short answer is that Spencer's financial circumstances had changed. The family had always lived beyond its means, and despite Earl George's personal piety and morality, and his record of public service, he was in his way as financially incompetent as his wastrel father. By the 1820s the crisis was severe, and it came to a head precisely in 1826 when the family was forced to leave its home at Wimbledon Park House. By now Spencer was an old man of 68. He had been born at Wimbledon and had lived there almost all his life. It must have been a terrible blow, and an enormous humiliation, to be forced to leave.

It is therefore hardly surprising that the fate of Penge Common was less of a priority for Spencer in 1826 than it had been in previous years. But his refusal to defend the Common sprang not just from his attention to pressing family business. All the signs are that he had reached some sort of financial accommodation with Cator: he had been bought off.

John Barwell Cator's 1826 Bill made much of a claim that Earl Spencer's father had granted 'paramount rights' over Penge Common to the Cator family. This is highly unlikely. In the first place, if such a promise were made, it must by definition have been made in or before 1783 when Earl John Spencer died. At this time, the head of the Cator family was John, John Barwell's uncle. But John Cator had no interest in Penge Common in or before 1783. His own lands were in Beckenham, not Penge, and he was at this time entirely taken up with building his new home and developing his circle of acquaintances. The person with the most obvious interest in Penge Common at this time was his neighbour John Morgan, but in 1783 even Morgan had not yet embarked on his long enclosure campaign. It beggars belief that John Cator could have acquired 'paramount rights' over Penge Common under the nose of his neighbour, and then sat quietly by over the following years, watching his neighbour try and try again to enclose that same piece of common land, never once mentioning that he himself already had rights over it. It is even more mysterious that Cator should have remained silent about these 'rights' when he submitted his own Enclosure Bill in 1797, only to encounter immediate and vigorous opposition from Earl George Spencer, the son of the man who had allegedly bestowed the 'rights' upon him.

The whole story about 'paramount rights' therefore looks like a fiction cooked up by John Barwell Cator in 1826. It is true that in 1826 Earl George Spencer endorsed that fiction. But as we have seen, by now he was aged, weary, short of money and emotionally distraught. The likeliest explanation for his acquiescence in the fiction is that he received in return some sort of accommodation – a pay-off. And from Cator's point of view it worked, in that it helped get his Enclosure Bill through Parliament.

Maybe it also served another purpose, as a form of family revenge by Cator upon Spencer himself. We have already remarked upon the enthusiasm with which Spencer opposed John Cator's Enclosure Bill back in 1797, and speculated that there may have been some personal motivation for this: aristocratic contempt for an upstart timber merchant getting ideas above his station, perhaps. If so, then John Barwell Cator's tale of 'paramount rights' may have been intended to achieve two aims: firstly to enclose the Common; and secondly to exact revenge upon the aristocrat who had used his Parliamentary influence to defeat Cator's uncle 30 years earlier, by purchasing his acquiescence in a lie. For a man like Spencer, with a reputation for public service and upright Christian integrity, it would have been deeply humiliating.

The Vestry's impertinent questions to Spencer and the Vicar about 'arrangements ... entered into ... with Mr. Cator ... ' now make sense. Such a letter could never have been written unless Vestry members themselves were convinced that Cator had in fact bought Spencer's support. And this meant that the Vicar of Battersea had been paid off too, since his living was entirely dependent on Spencer's patronage.

In May 1827 the Vestry met and noted that John Barwell Cator's Bill had been passed in the House of Commons, and was now in the Lords. It resolved that it was 'not expedient' to petition further, and that the Bill should be allowed to proceed unimpeded. The battle against enclosure was finally over.

Implementation

For 35 years the Crooked Billet near Penge Green had served as a coaching inn on the Beckenham-Dulwich road, and as a local meeting place. It was therefore a natural base for Richard Peyton, the Commissioner appointed to oversee the enclosure of Penge Common. In September and October 1827 he held three meetings at the Crooked Billet to hear claims from individuals with an interest in the enclosure.

He was, however, only prepared to consider claims in the form of individual property-rights backed up by title-deeds or other legal documentation. The poorest local residents were therefore excluded: their traditional rights to graze animals and gather fuel on the Common were backed up by no title-deeds, so they were not heard. But landowners, freeholders and others who could prove a claim to Peyton's satisfaction were put on the list for free allocation of former common land. Land which was not distributed in this way was sold at auctions, the first of which took place on 30 October 1827. The Vestry noted that the Common was being advertised as:

A very valuable Piece or Parcel of Land Freehold and Tithe Free situate on the west side of the Road leading from Beckenham to Dulwich and adjoining the Croydon Canal....

Those receiving land by allocation were William Fox of Croydon, William Booth of Sheffield, William Wilson of Sydenham, John Lawrie, and E.R. Adams, a local landowner who had opposed enclosure the year before. Cator acquired the largest single portion of land at auction; other slices were bought by Lawrie, Adams, and a group of property speculators from London: Messrs. Duikes, Wear, Siddiard, Gary and Sanderson.

Even now, with the land allocated to its new private owners, legal wrangles continued. The Vestry re-discovered its appetite for a scrap, and mounted a rearguard action, arguing that it was entitled to receive an award of land. Due to this and other disputes the enclosure was not finally implemented for another ten years. However, not everyone waited for the legal niceties. By 1837, 320 acres of common land were effectively enclosed – a premature and maybe even illegal act that can only have been the work of local landowners such as the Cators who presumably felt that they were too powerful to be challenged.

The privilege of land-ownership brought certain obligations. The new owners were obliged to contribute to the improvement of existing roads and the construction of new ones, and in doing this they gave shape to the road-pattern which we still see today. Some roads followed existing lines: Beckenham Road/Penge High Street along the old coaching road from Bromley; Croydon Road along an ancient trackway; Clay Lane at the lower end of what is now Anerley Road; and Penge Lane, Green Lane, and Kent House Road around the Crooked Billet and Penge Green. New link roads were also added: the missing section of the future Anerley Road was created by linking Vicar's Oak with Clay Lane; the future Maple Road was created on a line across the former Common from north-east to south-west; and a number of new roads were built in the Vicar's Oak/Westow Hill area.

These improvements to the road network meant that the Penge Enclosure overall was relatively expensive. Probably the new land-owners begrudged the money, but they had the compensation of knowing that their newly-acquired land was a sound investment. By the mid-1830s the Croydon Canal was on the brink of collapse, but its physical infrastructure, the canal bed itself, was already being eyed up by a group of railway entrepreneurs as the route for a line from London to Croydon. The canal had allowed bulk goods – including timber from Penge's woodland – to be shifted to market in London. Now the railway opened up the prospect of moving large numbers of people to and from the capital. Just as the canal had transformed Penge Common from a 'wasteland' into a source of commercial timber, so the railway would trans-form it into an area ripe for residential development.

The Vestry and the Common:
class struggle or parochial rivalry?

The enclosure of Penge Common was a single, tiny episode in a process of rural dispossession which had started centuries earlier, and which redefined land in England as a commodity, a saleable item of private property. The enforcement of this definition of landed property was a key element in the emergence of capitalist production and a capitalist class.

Does it therefore follow that the long battle over the Penge Enclosure was an episode of class struggle? The immediate ben-eficiaries were local gentry and middle-class incomers and specu-lators, who used their newly-acquired wealth for property devel-opment. Clearly, enclosure underwrote local capital accumula-tion. But does it necessarily follow that the opponents of enclo-sure therefore represented a social interest which was intrinsically anti-capitalist?

The organised opposition to the Penge Enclosure came from the Battersea Vestry, supported at key moments by their aristo-cratic patron, Earl Spencer. Spencer's class identity speaks for itself. The Vestry's members, meanwhile, were shop-keepers, merchants, small landowners, and respectable artisans. These

people had a high regard for private property-rights. Nor were
they opposed in principle to the enclosure of common land: their
own records show many instances where they nodded through
small-scale enclosures on Battersea Common – often benefiting
one or other of their own number – in exchange for a one-off
payment or a continuing income to the parish. They were in
addition committed moral guardians, enthusiastically pursuing
local ne'er-do-wells who failed to observe the sabbath; and – at
least until the betrayal of 1826 – they were generally deferential
towards Earl Spencer. To sum up, the Vestry showed no signs
of being a rallying point for radicals. On the contrary, it was a
gathering of pious, somewhat self-important and frequently self-
serving local worthies.

Why then did this Vestry, this conservative body wedded to
the principles of private property, put such energy into defend-
ing Penge Common – up to and including defiance of the law?
Dudley offers two explanations. His first is that the Vestry wished
to defend its own right to income from the Poor Rate. But on
this argument we would expect the Vestry to act as the foremost
champion of enclosure, because income from the Poor Rate was
generated not by unenclosed common land but by private property.

Dudley's second explanation is that the Vestry wished to protect the rights of Penge's poor parishioners to use the Common
for grazing and fuel-gathering. This of course is precisely how
the Vestry justified its actions, but we cannot simply take it at
face value. Defence of poor parishioners made for good rhetoric,
but it is difficult to take it seriously as a fundamental issue of
principle, when the same Vestry regularly approved enclosures in
Battersea itself which ignored the equivalent rights of Battersea's
own poor parishioners.

However, this very inconsistency points us towards a solution
to this problem. The Battersea Vestry held traditional common
rights to be of supreme importance in Penge, yet treated the same
rights with casual indifference on its own home ground. Why this
distinction? The key factor is surely Penge's physical separation

from Battersea, its status as a 'detached hamlet' of the parish, with the consequence that Penge's residents were not part of the Battersea-based social networks in which the Vestry was embedded.

If a respectable householder in Battersea cast a covetous eye on a patch of common land, he could sound out the Vestry's likely attitude by having a discreet word with any one its members, all of whom were neighbours. So long as he then submitted a suitably humble petition to the Churchwarden (a neighbour), and paid due respect to the corporate and individual self-importance of the Vestry and its other members (all neighbours), he would probably get his parcel of land.

However landowners in Penge were not part of this Battersea social circle and – if John Morgan is any guide – were less likely to appreciate the rules of the game. When Morgan made his first bid to enclose Penge Common he did so as an outsider, and what's more a particularly crude and heavy-handed outsider. Rather than submit a humble petition, he nailed a note to the church door asserting his claim. Rather than adopt a piece-meal approach, acquiring common land bit by bit over a period of time, he laid claim to the whole of the Common from the start. It is almost as if his actions were calculated to drive the Battersea-based members of the Vestry together by emphasising his own status as an outsider; and to focus their attention on the Vestry's corporate and traditional rights by refusing to respect its procedures. In effect, he drove them onto a patch of moral high ground which turned out to be remarkably convenient for them. He gave them Penge Common as a symbol around which they could unite to demonstrate publicly their commitment to the traditional rights of the parish and the defence of the poor, without threatening their own immediate self-interest as property-owners in Battersea.

The battle over the Penge Enclosure was not therefore a contest between different social classes with fundamentally different interests at stake. It was rather a contest between rival groups of property-owners. Morgan, Scott and Cator, from the sub-rural gentry, sought to enclose the Common to enhance their own wealth and power. The members of the Battersea Vestry, from the sub-urban middle class, sought to defend the traditional rights of parish and Vestry, from which they drew local influence and status. Both groups drew their legitimacy from the established social order.

Sources

Battersea Vestry, Minutes of Proceedings, held in Battersea Library, Local History Department, Lavender Hill, London.

Cobbett, William, 1967. *Rural Rides*, Penguin, Hamondsworth.

Corbett Anderson, D., 1889. *Croydon Inclosure*. Private publication, Croydon.

Dudley, M.R. 1980. *The Parliamentary Enclosure Movement: Penge Hamlet, c. 1780-1860.* St. Catherine's College, Cambridge.

Filmer, J.L., 'The Norman Family of Bromley Common', in *Bromley Local History*, no. 2, 1977. Local History Society for the London Borough of Bromley.

Hasted, E., 1983, *The History & Topography of Kent: Pt. 111, Beckenham, Bromley*, reprinted from 2nd edition of 1797, P.M.E. Erwood, Sidcup.

Inman, Eric R. & Tonkin, Nancy, 1993, *Beckenham*, Phillimore, Chichester.

Inwood, Stephen, 1998, *A History of London*, Macmillan, London.

Knowlden, Patricia. 1977. Village into Suburb' in *Bromley Local History*, no. 2. Local History Society for the London Borough of Bromley.

Linebaugh, Peter, 1993. *The London Hanged*, Penguin, Harmondsworth.

Pearson, John, 2000. *Blood Royal*. Harper Collins, London.

Porter, Roy. 1996. *London, a Social History*. Penguin, Harmondsworth.

Pullen, Doris E. 1971. *Penge*, Able Publications, Knebworth.

Rackham, Oliver. 1986. *The History of the Countryside*. Phoenix Press, London.

Taylor, Bessie. 1965. *Bromley, Beckenham & Penge, Kent, since 1750.* Department of Geography, Birkbeck College, London.
Victoria Histories of the Counties of England: Surrey, 1967. Reprint of 1912 edition. Dawson, London.

CROYDON CANAL. *VIEW IN PENGE WOOD*

London, Published as the Act directs, by R. Wilkinson, No. 58 Cornhill.

Chapter 6
'Speculations of a profitable traffic': the Croydon Canal

Beginnings

It is possible to live all your life in South London and not know that a working canal once ran between the Thames and Croydon. A canal is by definition an ambitious undertaking, an artificial waterway cut through the landscape, and yet the Croydon Canal seems to have left only a few remnants: a short stretch of water in a concrete culvert in Anerley; odd street-names such as Canal Walk; and South Norwood Lake, which began life as its reservoir. And yet there is one more legacy left by the Canal, a highly visible and significant one, in the form of a major railway line from London Bridge to West Croydon. For long stretches the line runs along the former canal bed. The near-invisibility of the Croydon Canal today is therefore a sort of back-handed historical compliment, in that it was such a crucial achievement in transport engineering that it was seized upon, recycled and thoroughly absorbed by a whole new transport technology.

The rationale for the Croydon Canal was rooted in the commercial and political circumstances of the late eighteenth and early nineteenth centuries.

In the late 1780s and early 1790s more than fifty new canal projects were authorised throughout the country: 1792 has been described as a year of 'Canal Mania' comparable to the railway mania of 1845. New roads – privately-financed 'turnpikes' – were also being built at the same time. However Parliament had laid down different rules for these different ventures. Turnpike trusts were tightly regulated and subject to controls on the amount of interest they could receive. Investors in canals, however, were allowed to reap their profits directly and in full once they had established their companies with Parliament's permission. Canal projects were therefore relatively difficult and expensive to get off the ground – but once approved, and if successful, they delivered healthy profits to their investors.

In 1799 a coalition of aristocrats, gentry, bankers and engineers launched the construction of a commercial canal from the Surrey Docks to Croydon. The proposal had a clear commercial logic. It was intended to improve communications and trade between Croydon – a thriving market town of about 6,000 people – and London. Croydon offered a solid trade in bulk goods such as cereals, timber, market garden produce and lime, but the area's roads were notorious. Meanwhile, along the south bank of the Thames, a boom in dock building was under way. Several new docks were built in the early years of the nineteenth century, both commercial (the Surrey Docks at Rotherhithe) and naval (the Royal Victualling Yard at Deptford). Both ends of the projected Canal therefore offered prospects for healthy trade, and the Canal's backers believed that anyone who could provide a new and more rapid means of communication between them should make a handsome profit. They aimed in text-book fashion to reduce turnover time, to annihilate space by time, through the application of technology.

There was also another factor in play. Despite the country's buoyant economic growth and trade, this was a period of repeated military and diplomatic setbacks. In the 1770s Britain lost its American colonies – an enormous blow in terms of resources and prestige. In 1789 the French Revolution took place, and from 1793 Europe was swept into a rolling tide of revolutionary wars. Over the following years a series of ineffective alliances was stitched together to try to contain the French: all of them were bankrolled by Britain, and all of them failed. By 1803 Britain was faced by a financial crisis which forced the Government to take the unprecedented step of imposing an income tax, and by the very real prospect of French invasion. The country's army at this time was of little use: it had not yet been rebuilt by Wellington, and was puny, amateurish and badly-led, no match for Napoleon's well-drilled and confident troops. But the Royal Navy was another matter. It was on the Navy that the country pinned its hopes.

The promoters of the Croydon Canal were alive to this acute national crisis, and saw their project as an exercise in national salvation. The country's defence rested upon the Royal Navy, and the effectiveness of the Navy relied upon good communications and supply lines between London and the key naval base at Portsmouth. And yet the only way of travelling from London to Portsmouth was over appalling country roads, or out along the Thames and back round the south coast. A canal from London to Portsmouth would create a direct link.

In the eyes of its backers, a canal to Croydon was perfectly placed to act as the first stage of the much bigger project of a canal to Portsmouth. But it was not the only such project: rival London-to-Portsmouth routes were also being mooted based on the Surrey Iron Railway, and on a new canal link between the rivers Wey and Arun.

Building the Canal

The key backers of the Croydon Canal project were landowners with property on or close to its proposed route. Lords Gwyder, Auckland and Russell lent their names to the list of sponsors in 1799, and thus gave it an air of aristocratic respectability, but of these only Lord Gwyder actually put in any money. Meanwhile, John Morgan and John Scott, the two key landowners in Penge, each invested £500 – the maximum permissible individual investment. Support also came from leading City bankers, Sir Francis Baring and Sir Benjamin Hammett.

Building a canal is a daunting engineering exercise. The details of local geography take on enormous significance. Any feature which affects the canal's width, or the supply of water, or the need for locks, will necessarily affect its carrying-capacity and the speed at which barges can progress along it, and will therefore impact upon the all-important question of turnover time. There were long arguments between the Company's owners and engineers about the best route for the Croydon Canal.

The first engineer, Dodd, favoured a route of least resistance along the Pool and Ravensbourne river valleys. His canal would have looped eastwards from Croydon to link up with these rivers, and then north from Beckenham and through Catford towards the Thames. The advantage of this route was that it would run along an existing river valley without any climbs or descents. This meant it would be relatively easy to build, and once built it would have no time-consuming locks to pass through so that journey-time would be relatively short. The disadvantage was that the Ravensbourne is only a small river, so that the Canal would necessarily be narrow, restricting the size of the barges able to use it. This might have been good enough if the canal were intended only for trade between Croydon and London, but the Company's backers were committed to the grand vision of a Portsmouth extension. Dodd's modest proposal would have closed off this option from the start, and his plan was rejected.

A new engineer, John Rennie, was brought in. Rennie was to give rise to a great engineering dynasty: he and his sons would win fame and respect as some of the great builders of the railway age. But in 1800 John Rennie still had a name to make. His approach to the Croydon Canal was to seize the high ground. Instead of following the river valleys, Rennie proposed a route along elevated sections of South London's hills, from Croydon via Selhurst to Penge Common, then to Sydenham and Forest Hill, and on to New Cross, Deptford and Rotherhithe. The disadvantage of this route was that it meant building a string of locks as the canal followed the rising and falling contours of the landscape, making travel times painfully slow. But balanced against this was the advantage that a canal along this route could be relatively broad, allowing the passage of large barges. This had two consequences: it increased the overall carrying capacity; and it kept open the prospect of an extension to the naval dockyard at Portsmouth. This was the chosen route.

In 1801 the Company got the go-ahead from Parliament, which passed an Act for the building of the Canal, and empowered the Company to buy or rent any land it needed. However in the same year – as if in a spirit of mischief – Parliament also gave approval to the Surrey Iron Railway. Promoted by a group of Wandle valley industrialists, this was a horse-drawn railway running along the Wandle river valley from Croydon to Wandsworth. It was a direct challenge to the Croydon Canal, with exactly the same commercial rationale – an improved transport link between Croydon and London.

Of the two rival projects the Iron Railway got off to a much quicker start. With its straightforward route, and its relatively simple technology, it took just two years to build the Railway and open for business. The Canal Company however faced problems on an altogether different scale. Any canal poses major challenges in civil engineering and water-management, but the Croydon Canal faced in addition the particular problems created by its chosen route, with a total of twenty-eight locks to be built between New Cross and Croydon.

In 1804 and 1805, as hundreds of labourers toiled to carve out the Canal's route across South London, and with the Iron Railway already doing brisk business a few miles to the west, the Canal's backers must have had serious second thoughts. In 1804 their formal proposal for a Portsmouth extension was rejected by Parliament. This must have been a great disappointment, but they may have comforted themselves with the thought that they could always revise the route and try again. However, in 1805 an event occurred which fundamentally undermined the whole proposal: Nelson won the Battle of Trafalgar. The urgency of the Portsmouth link had always rested on the threat of French invasion. Trafalgar removed that threat, and thus undermined half the rationale for the Croydon Canal.

However, the project was too far advanced to be abandoned, and the Canal finally opened for business in October 1809. The Company marked the opening in style, with a procession of barges which started at Sydenham and ended at Croydon – thus avoiding most of the locks. It was accompanied by a 21-gun salute, a chorus of 'God Save the King', and a banquet at *The Greyhound*. The report of the day records that the Canal's proprietors '... (testified) their joy that all their speculations of a profitable traffic were now realised' and at their banquet the toast was: 'The union of the River Thames and the English Channel through the Croydon Canal'. Clearly the dream of a Portsmouth link lived on – at least for purposes of public consumption.

The Canal's route through Penge more or less followed the line of the existing railway from Sydenham to Penge West, Anerley and Norwood Junction. Its most committed local backer was John Scott, owner of Penge Place from 1801 to 1813. Scott was one of the original investors in the Canal Company, and he was responsible for building Penge Wharf. This was a key factor in the Canal's overall commercial strategy. It was the point of distribution from which Beckenham, Bromley and other parts of northeast Kent would now receive coal and other bulk goods at greatly reduced prices; and it was the point of despatch for timber from Penge's woods to make its way up to London.

We saw in Chapter 5 that in the final stages of the long battle over the enclosure of Penge Common, the Battersea Vestry alleged that in 1812 Scott had received a payment from the Canal Company. The implication was that he had taken this money as payment for several acres of Common land acquired by the Company in 1802, which in turn would have implied that he regarded the Common as his private property. However, timing suggests that any payment received by Scott in 1812 is more likely to have been connected with the recent construction of Penge Wharf, rather than the acquisition of Common land ten years earlier. The Wharf was after all a major commercial asset for the Canal as a whole, so there would be nothing unusual in the Canal Company reimbursing him.

Whatever the truth of the matter, despite the money invested by Scott and others, and despite the high hopes and celebrations which marked its opening, the Canal was never a paying commercial proposition. Its constant inclines and descents, and its numerous locks, simply made it too slow. It carved out a modest business for itself over the next twenty years ferrying bulk goods: stone, lime, fullers earth and timber to London; coal to Croydon. But its investors never got their money back. The only cold comfort available to them was that as their own money drained away, they were at least taking business from the Surrey Iron Railway and dragging it down with them.

Its disappointing performance in freight transport may explain why the Croydon Canal also promoted itself as a leisure amenity. Within a few years of its opening, engravings were being produced which show it meandering through a stereotypically bucolic countryside, populated by simple rustic folk, its character as a working industrial canal deliberately obscured. Penge was promoted as a particularly charming spot: one well-known scene claims to portray the Canal as it passes through 'Penge Forest' – a flattering but inaccurate term for the Common – and there was said to be especially good fishing at Penge Wharf.

But these attempts to promote leisure use, fishing and day-trippers could never make up for the commercial shortfall. By the late 1820s the Croydon Canal Company was in deep trouble, and by 1830 a nominal £100 share had fallen in value to 2/-.

Just at this time there was, ironically, a sudden revival of interest in the idea of a major canal from London to Portsmouth. Between 1825 and 1828 three routes were proposed for a Grand Imperial Ship Canal, one of them promoted by the sons of John Rennie, the Croydon Canal's engineer. However, the Grand Imperial project collapsed, partly under the weight of its own financial ambition, and also because by this time a modest London-to-Portsmouth waterway actually existed, by means of the Wey Navigation, Wey and Arun Canal, River Arun, and Portsmouth & Arundel Canal.

The Croydon Canal finally shut up shop in 1836. But its legacy as a transport route carved across the landscape of South London lives on. Even before it closed, its route was being surveyed by the London & Croydon Railway Company, which went on to buy up the Canal Company's assets for about one third of the cost of its construction. At a stroke the railway company thus acquired all the value embodied in the canal's cuttings and embankments and gradients. Just three years later trains were operating along a new line from London Bridge to Croydon, a line which for significant stretches simply ran along the former canal bed. Thus the abject failure of one transport enterprise underwrote and made possible runaway success in another.

Sources

Dudley, M.R. 1980. *The Parliamentary Enclosure Movement: Penge Hamlet, c. 1780-1860.* St. Catherine's College, Cambridge.

Living History Publications, 1986. *Retracing Canals from Croydon to Camberwell,* Living History Publications, East Grinstead.

Porter, Roy. 1996. *London, a Social History.* Penguin, Harmondsworth.

Taylor, Bessie. 1965. *Bromley, Beckenham & Penge, Kent, since 1750.* Department of Geography, Birkbeck College, London.

Vine, P.A.L. *London's Lost Route to the Sea.* David & Charles, Newton Abbot, 1986.

Wandle Group, The. 1997. *The Wandle Guide,* London Borough of Sutton Leisure Services, Sutton.

White, Ken. 1989. *The Croydon Canal and its Neighbours.* Ken White (privately published), London.

Chapter 7
'The crowning work': the railways

According to Marx the railways were the 'crowning work' of nineteenth century industrial capitalism. They were its shock technology. The railways tore open whole continents, laying bare people, land and raw materials to the limitless appetites of capital. And Coleman argues that the sheer breath-taking scope of the enterprise was just as evident in England as it was in the vast expanses of America or India:

> Only the cathedrals before were so vast in idea: nothing before was so vast in scale.... As a feat of engineering, the M1 is nothing compared to the London and Birmingham Railway, completed 120 years before.

Railway lines and railway stations are so familiar to us today that we take them utterly for granted. And yet the very structure of urban South London, the sinuous routes followed by the rails, the ways in which they carve the territory up into discrete parcels, the cuttings and viaducts – all these marks on the present-day landscape are the legacy of the back-breaking labour of thousands of workers, and the ruthless ambition of the commercial railway companies which put them to work.

These companies needed certain preconditions before starting to build their lines. They needed access to continuous corridors of land over which the rails were to run. This meant that they needed to acquire the land at an acceptable price, and to override the rights of other property owners who might be affected by the filthy, disruptive, dangerous job of building the line. Dickens witnessed it at first hand:

Houses were knocked down; streets were broken through and stopped; deep pits and trenches dug in the ground; enormous heaps of earth and clay thrown up; buildings that were undermined and shaking, propped by great beams of wood.... Everywhere were bridges that led nowhere; thoroughfares that were wholly impassable; Babel towers of chimneys, wanting half their height; temporary wooden houses and enclosures in the most unlikely situations... In short, the yet unfinished and unopened Railroad was in progress ....

This physical upheaval was brought about, of course, by the hard work of the railway workers, or 'navvies'. The term 'navvy' comes from 'navigator'. It was first applied in the eighteenth century to the men who constructed the canals, and passed on in the next century to those who built the railways. Navvies were the workers who did all the hardest and most dangerous work in railway construction: the blasting and cutting. They made up an entire nomadic society of their own. They lived in temporary shacks or shanty-towns which followed the railway tracks, each of which commonly had a complement of common-law wives and prostitutes alongside the men. Navvies were so famous for their pagan ways – weddings were often accomplished by leaping the broomstick – that a whole body of missionaries grew up to bring the word of God to these heathens in darkest England. They were famous also for their near-constant drunkenness – actively encouraged by their employers as a rough and ready means of social control – and for their fighting.

In short, the railways brought with them disruption and danger, and the men who ran the railway companies knew that they could only get away with inflicting this outrage on their fellow citizens if they could win the active support, or at least the benign oversight, of the state. They worked hard to win it, and in general they succeeded.

They also chose their routes with care. They needed routes capable of generating sufficient traffic and income to make the whole operation profitable. But they could not afford simply to respond passively to the pattern of settlement as it existed before the rails were laid. They sought instead to be active agents in their own destiny, creating facts on the ground which would generate traffic, revenue and thus dividends for their many avid shareholders. In choosing new routes, the railway companies were acutely aware of their role as catalysts, encouraging builders and investors to create new suburbs, and even whole new towns, along their brave new lines.

Railways were pioneers of capitalism in another way as well. Railway stocks were the first to mobilise significant levels of investment from the general public through the creation of joint stock companies, and this in turn dragged the Stock Exchange away from its longstanding focus on government bonds. Before the railways, the technical innovations of the Industrial Revolution had been financed by individual engineers and entrepreneurs, or by their families or local patrons. Afterwards, the savings of the nation as a whole were, in principle, made available.

However, all these goals had to be achieved within the limits of the technology. The great advantage of the railway as a means of transport is the lack of friction between wheel and rail: it is this which allows engines to pull great loads at high speeds. But once a train encounters a slope, its technical advantage turns against it as lack of friction becomes lack of traction. This prosaic reality had major implications in South London whose hills are not particularly high, but are in many places fairly steep. As a result, tunnels were bored, and cuttings were carved, and viaducts were built, and embankments were raised, and a whole new urban landscape took shape across South London.

The London & Croydon Railway Co.

The first line to pass through Penge was the London & Croydon Railway Company (LCR) line from the new terminus at London Bridge to West Croydon, which opened in 1839. Its commercial logic was the same as that of the Croydon Canal or the Surrey Iron Railway: a transport link between Croydon and London.

However, it was an advance on the Iron Railway in that it used the new technology of steam; and it had a further advantage in that it inherited the route of the canal, thus benefiting from the enormous capital cost of construction invested – and lost – by the Canal Company. The LCR purchased the Canal for just over £40,000, less than a third of the cost of construction.

Penge's potential was plain to see. The enclosure of the Commons was complete; all local land was now in the hands of private landowners. They had every incentive to use it profitably, and they were clear that with the arrival of the railway the most profitable use was not for agriculture – the original rationale for enclosure – but for development as a select residential suburb. A building programme of substantial upper-middle-class villas began in the 1830s: about 50 houses were under construction in the early 1840s.

However, when the railway service began in 1839 there were still not enough local residents to provide a critical mass of passengers. Penge's population at this time was about 270. Penge Wharf' had been replaced just across the road by Penge Station (now Penge West) but it closed almost as soon as it had opened, for lack of business.

Anerley Station, a mile down the track, was a different story. The land here was owned by William Sanderson, one of the speculators who had purchased land at auction when the Penge enclosure was finally settled. He presumably knew that the railway was coming and he seems to have chosen his site carefully. His land consisted of several acres of wood-heathland, including a loop of defunct Canal which defined a sort of artificial island right next to the new railway line.

The LCR never intended to build a station at Anerley. However Sanderson persuaded them to do so by giving them the land for free, and he then turned the little island into 'Anerley Gardens', a rustic pleasure garden complete with Swiss Cottage, bandstand and maze. At one level Anerley Gardens was simply a modest leisure amenity like numerous other spas and pleasure gardens. But at another level Sanderson was a genuine entrepreneurial pioneer.

He saw that railways had the potential to deposit large numbers of passengers at desirable locations. And he realised that if he could make his own railside property into a desirable location, sufficiently amusing or enticing to persuade passengers to get off the train, he could transform them from fare-paying passengers of the railway company into fee-paying customers of his own.

From the 1850s the Gardens were overshadowed by the sheer size, scale and grandeur of the Crystal Palace – the pleasure garden to end all pleasure gardens – less than a mile away. But it was Sanderson who pioneered the idea of exploiting commercial mass transport to create the conditions for commercial mass recreation.

Our primary interest here has been local, focusing on the impact of the railway as it passed through Penge and Anerley. But this was just part of a bigger picture, because the London to Croydon line was one of the very earliest passenger lines in the country, a genuine experiment in the concept of commuting by railway. The LCR started operating in 1839, just three years after London's very first railway service to Greenwich from London Bridge. London Bridge Station itself only opened in 1836, and was at this time London's only railway terminus for South London and indeed for the whole of South-East England. Another twelve years would pass before Waterloo Station was built; and twenty-five years would pass before all the other terminus stations serving South London and the South-East appeared – Blackfriars, Cannon Street, Charing Cross and Victoria. In the middle decades of the nineteenth century London Bridge Station pioneered local and commuter railways for the city and its suburbs, and the LCR was one of its earliest experiments.

The London Brighton & South Coast Railway Co.

In 1846 the LCR merged with the London and Brighton Railway to form the London Brighton & South Coast Railway Company (LBSCR). This was the height of the great railway boom. The railways were the fastest-growing industrial sector in Britain; Britain was the greatest industrial power in the world; and London and south-east England was then, as now, its core region of economic growth. So the LBSCR was from its inception an enormously powerful player: a leading force in the fastest growing industry, in the fastest growing region, in the fastest growing economy in the world.

The company's significance for Penge sprang not only from its acquisition of the London to Croydon line, but also from its close connection with the Crystal Palace. The Crystal Palace was the offspring of the Great Exhibition in Hyde Park in 1851. The Exhibition was a stunning success not just in terms of visitor numbers or public acclaim, but also because of the building which housed it. Joseph Paxton's light, elegant, pre-fabricated glass and iron structure was a triumph and made him into a national hero. Even while it was still in Hyde Park it acquired the nickname 'Crystal Palace' – the name was coined by *Punch* magazine to poke fun – but it caught on and was taken up as a mark of honour.

However, despite the Exhibition's success, it was always intended to have a limited life span. Paxton wanted the building to remain in Hyde Park as a 'Winter Park and Garden under Glass' but his argument failed. The Palace's owners, railway engineering contractors Fox and Henderson, were instructed to dismantle it.

But Paxton would not give up. He was determined to hold on to his celebrity status, which he realised was inseparable from the Crystal Palace building. If it couldn't stay in Hyde Park, the obvious solution was to reconstruct it somewhere else: since it was pre-fabricated this was perfectly possible. But he needed a suitable site, and he needed partners and investors who for their own reasons might support such a venture.

It didn't take long to identify the railway industry as the most likely source of support. It was no accident that a railway engineering company, Fox and Henderson, had won the contract to build the original Hyde Park Palace: in the mid nineteenth century, the railways were the cutting edge of technological innovation and engineering technique. Paxton therefore reckoned that the railway industry was the obvious place to seek support for a successor to the Hyde Park Palace. He approached the LBSCR to seek its backing for a new venture, the Crystal Palace Company.

The LBSCR agreed to become the majority shareholder in the Crystal Palace Company, and suddenly things started to happen. Firstly, one of the LBSCR's Directors, Samuel Laing MP, became the Chairman of the Crystal Palace Company and the project's chief advocate in Parliament. Secondly, the Company now had the resources to negotiate the purchase of the Hyde Park Palace from Fox and Henderson. And finally, the LBSCR came up with a new site. Another of its Directors, Leo Schuster, happened to be the owner of Penge Place. He agreed to join Laing on the Board of the Crystal Palace Company, on condition that the Company bought Penge Place from him and used it as the location for the new Crystal Palace.

The LBSCR's support for Paxton was not, of course, an act of charity. The company saw the project as a gigantic money-spinner on two fronts. Firstly, they reckoned that it would generate profits for them as customers paid their entrance fees at the turnstile. And secondly, they calculated that they would also make money from the railway tickets bought by those same people, as they travelled to and from the Crystal Palace on the new railway line that the Company intended to build specifically for the purpose. Overall, it is no exaggeration to say that the Crystal Palace was a creature of the railway industry. It would never have happened without the railway industry. Its very conception as a commercial venture was underpinned by the judgements and ambitions of railway entrepreneurs.

And yet we should also recognise that these entrepreneurs were taking a gamble. Although the railways were expanding at a phenomenal rate, there was no guarantee that any given line would be a success: many lines failed and the companies that built them went bust. In fact the whole idea of urban and suburban commuter lines was still controversial in the 1850s: there was a powerful school of thought which held that the railway was by definition a long-distance mode of transport, and that within cities it would never compete with the horse. These views may seem timid and wrong-headed to us, but they were based in observable reality in the 1850s. In 1854, the year in which the Crystal Palace opened in South London, railways still delivered fewer than 10,000 workers to the City every day. Many more came by horse-drawn omnibus and steamboat, and the vast majority – 200,000 or so – came by foot. Even ten years later, some commuters still travelled every day on horseback from Croydon to the City.

Paxton, Laing, Schuster and their colleagues were aware of the risk that they were taking, and they used all the means available to them to minimise it. In particular, Laing used his influence in Parliament to secure the passage of an extraordinarily supportive Act. Firstly, it authorised the LBSCR to construct a new spur line from Jolly Sailor Station (now Norwood Junction) to the Crystal Palace site: initially this was used to ferry building materials, and then it served as a passenger route to deliver paying customers to Crystal Palace Station. Secondly, Parliament authorised an enlargement of London Bridge Station: this was justified as wise anticipation of the extra traffic which the project was expected to generate, but of course it also served as a positive inducement to such traffic. Finally, Parliament specified that special low fares should be charged on the new Crystal Palace line. This may have reduced the LBSCR's income per ticket, but at the same time it tended to increase the overall number of tickets sold, and thus increased the number of visitors delivered to the site itself, where its subsidiary Crystal Palace Company was waiting to take their money again in the form of entrance fees.

Superficially, the relationship between the Crystal Palace and the railway was similar to that between Anerley Gardens and the railway: both used it to deliver paying customers to their gates. But there was a qualitative difference. Anerley Gardens was essentially opportunistic: the railway was coming through anyway, Sanderson saw that this would confer new value upon adjacent land, and he moved adroitly to exploit the opportunity. The Crystal Palace however was on a different scale, not just in the sense that it was bigger and covered more acres, but in the sense that its owners built entirely new railway lines, and secured the active support of the state, in order to bring the venture into being. The Crystal Palace is a neat illustration of some of the enduring realities of capitalist enterprise. It was an entrepreneurial initiative in that it was the outcome of a calculated commercial risk by private investors; and at the same time it was a political initiative, utterly reliant on the active support of the state. There is no contradiction here: the ability to play politics and win the support of the state has always been a key entrepreneurial skill.

The London Chatham & Dover Railway Company

The Crystal Palace was very much the creature of the LBSCR, but in 1862 an Act of Parliament authorised one of the company's rivals, the London Chatham & Dover Railway Company (LCDR), to run a second line to the Palace from Peckham Rye. The LBSCR already had their own Station on Anerley Hill, so the new terminus – at the top of the hill alongside Crystal Palace Parade – was called Crystal Palace High Level.

The new line was initiated by the LCDR during a period of truce with the LBSCR, when both companies found it advantageous to cooperate in order to realise their different ambitions. By standing aside and letting the High Level project go ahead, the LBSCR obtained LCDR acquiescence to its own projects elsewhere in South London, including a loop line from London Bridge to the new terminus at Victoria. It also calculated that, in its capacity as majority shareholder in the Crystal Palace, it would ultimately benefit from a new railway line which brought in more paying customers.

The Crystal Palace High Level line opened in 1865, with a terminus which aimed to set a new standard in railway style and architecture: craftsmen were brought in from Italy to fashion its Byzantine crypt. It also revealed the Victorian obsession with class: not only were there separate carriages on the trains, but also separate subways from the Station to the Crystal Palace, so that First Class passengers could arrive and enter without having to mix at any point with Second or Third Class passengers.

Despite all this lavish investment the High Level line turned out to be an object lesson in the high-risk nature of nineteenth century railway investment. It was a commercial failure because it failed to observe one of the basic rules of capitalist railways: make sure there are plenty of locations along the line capable of delivering fare-paying passengers. On its way to Peckham the High Level line passed through Dulwich Woods, a municipal cemetery, and a scatter of large houses. While pleasantly picturesque, this was not much good for generating passing trade. The front-company set up by the LCDR went through a boardroom revolt in 1874, and a year later it was formally merged back into LCDR's wider operation.

At the same time as the High Level line was being built, the LCDR was also busy on a quite separate project which led to yet another line running through Penge. This line was the company's attempt to cut in on the lucrative boat-train business, which linked London to the cross-Channel ferries arriving at Dover. The South Eastern Railway Company (SER), already ran a service from London Bridge, but the LCDR aimed to trump them with an entirely new and shorter route from Victoria. This line ran through Brixton to Herne Hill, and then through a new tunnel under Sydenham Hill to Penge, Beckenham, Bromley and on to Dover.

Although its primary rationale was to service the boat-trains, in its early stages the line ran through a broad swathe of fast-growing suburbs offering rich commuter pickings. And once built, the line itself acted as a catalyst for the further expansion of these suburbs. Penge itself is a good illustration. Penge East Station opened in 1863, contributing to a local house-building boom which peaked during that decade.

In our own time, the line has once again provided a mix of commuter and international services – the international dimension being provided by Eurostar on its way from Waterloo to the channel tunnel.

The South Eastern Railway Company

We saw in Chapter 3 that the social impact of railway lines during this period was often brutal. The promise of the railway companies was that their lines opened up new and appealing suburban possibilities and in 'greenfield' areas this might be true: Penge's early growth in the 1840s was made possible largely by the advent of the London to Croydon railway. But when new lines were driven through existing residential areas, the result could be very different. A new railway line might claim to provide improved transport links to an exclusive upper-middle-class suburb, but in doing so it might also open up access to lower-middle-class and working-class incomers, and thus undermine or destroy the area's social character. Clapham is the classic example of this, as we have already seen.

However, this outcome was not inevitable. In some cases, where new lines were driven through existing residential areas, local power-brokers fought back against the railway companies. The so-called 'Mid-Kent' line in Penge is one example.

This line was developed in the early 1860s by the SER via a front company, the ludicrously mis-named Mid-Kent Railway Company, in alliance with a group of property developers. On its way from Lewisham to Addiscombe, the Mid-Kent line passed through land on the Penge-Beckenham border which was owned by the Cator family. The Cators were at this time in the process of developing the 'Cator Estate' as an exclusive, prestigious, upper-middle-class development. They were concerned that the arrival of the railway would lower the tone of the neighbourhood by disturbing the peace of the local residents, and by encouraging unwanted visitors from less respectable areas.

The Cators were simply too powerful to be ignored or over-ridden by the Mid-Kent Company, and they forced it to restrict train services on Sundays, and to plant trees and shrubs to hide the line from sight of the houses. In return they agreed to subsidise the construction costs of New Beckenham Station. The line opened in 1864. Parts of the route are used today by the service from London Bridge to Hayes, and parts by the Croydon Tramlink.

Sources

Anthony, John. 1973. *Joseph Paxton*. Shire Publications Ltd., Princes Risborough.

Beaver, Patrick. 1986. *The Crystal Palace*, Phillimore & Co. Ltd., Chichester.

Census of Great Britain 1841. (Penge enumeration tables).

Coleman, Terry. 1968. *The Railway Navvies*. Penguin, Harmondsworth

Croydon Natural History & Scientific Society (CNHSS), 1979. *Victorian Croydon Illustrated*, CNHSS Ltd., Croydon.

Dickens, Charles. 1998. 'Dombey and Son' in *Victorian Masterworks*, Magic Mouse Multimedia (CD-ROM).

Dudley, M.R. 1980. *The Parliamentary Enclosure Movement: Penge Hamlet, c. 1780-1860*. St. Catherine's College, Cambridge.

Friends of the Great North Wood, 1995, *From the Nun's Head to the Screaming Alice*.

Gilbert, Bob. 1991. *The Green London Way*. Lawrence & Wishart, London.

Inwood, Stephen, 1998, *A History of London*, Macmillan, London.

Jackson, Alan. 1999. *London's Local Railways*. Capital Transport Publishing, Harrow Weald.

Marx, Karl. 1979. 'Letter to Danielson, 10/4/1879' in De La Haye, Yves (ed.), *Marx and Engels on the Means of Communication*, International General, New York.

Porter, Roy. 1996. *London, a Social History*. Penguin, Harmondsworth.

Reeves, Graham. 1986. *Palace of the People*. Bromley Library Service, Bromley.

Scott, Mick. 1995. *Crystal Palace, Penge and Anerley*. Alan Sutton Publishing Ltd., Stroud.

Sheppard, Francis, 1998. *London: A History*, Oxford University Press, Oxford.

Taylor, Bessie. 1965. *Bromley, Beckenham & Penge, Kent, since 1750*. Department of Geography, Birkbeck College, London.

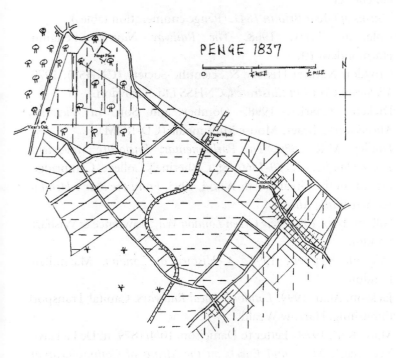

PENGE 1837

0 ¼ MILE ½ MILE

N

Penge Place

Vicar's Oak

Penge Wharf

Crooked Billet

Royal Watermen's and Lightermen's Almshouses, Penge. c.1890

King William IV Naval Asylum, Penge Lane, Penge

North Surrey District School

Chapter 8
'Opulent residents with elegant mansions':
An early Victorian suburb

By the late 1830s Penge was ripe for growth. The Commons enclosure was a fact of law and was becoming a fact on the ground. The Croydon Canal had failed its own shareholders, but for a while it had helped local landowners get their produce to market. And more significantly, it had accomplished a major feat of civil engineering, laying down a transport corridor across South London which the London and Croydon Railway Company could now exploit.

This was an attractive, up-and-coming area, which started to draw in well-connected and prosperous families with links to the City and the Court. And having decided to settle here, these families saw it as their right and duty to give both civic and moral leadership. In doing so they identified with a wider trend in society because this period was the heyday of the Clapham Sect, the self-appointed clique of businessmen and bankers which set out to tutor their fellows on the virtues of upper-class Christian duty.

The building of Penge Chapel provided the first outlet for this new local mood of civic duty and philanthropy. For centuries, the God-fearing residents of Penge had wrestled with the dilemma that their strict religious duty was to attend the parish church in Battersea, which was several miles away, although a perfectly serviceable alternative was available just along the road at Beckenham. In practice, the parish of Beckenham therefore looked after Penge's pastoral needs for which it received a fee from the parish of Battersea. In the 1830s this took the form of a visit to Penge hamlet by the curate of Beckenham every Sunday evening, to hold a makeshift service in one of the local cottages.

By 1837 this arrangement had come to be regarded as unsatis-
factory. A committee was established to build a local chapel, on
which the Cators were naturally well represented. Colonel W.
Cator represented the family interest, and Albert Cator made
land available at the corner of Croydon Road and Penge High
Street for a price of £35.

The Chapel was closely followed by another philanthropic
project, the Watermens Almshouses. This was initiated in 1839
by John Dudin-Brown, a well-connected City businessman and
local landowner. Dudin-Brown was on the governing body of
the Watermans & Lightermans Company, the ancient City Guild
whose members used to provide ferry services on the Thames.
From the mid eighteenth century they had been fighting a losing
battle, as more and more bridges were built across the river, each
of which directly reduced their trade. Dudin-Brown set out to
build almshouses for the surviving retired freemen of the company, and he felt that the quiet, respectable environment of Penge
would be ideal. He personally donated a parcel of land next to the
Crooked Billet, and he raised funds by drawing on his social connections, including King William IV's widow Queen Adelaide,
who donated 100 guineas. The almshouses, built in an idiosyn-
cratic mock-Tudor style, opened in 1841.

Penge at this point was therefore the very model of an up-
and-coming residential suburb: semi-rural, quietly fashionable,
appealing to well-heeled residents seeking to combine a secluded
family life with easy access to the City. It boasted a railway station
and a new chapel, its new almshouses enjoyed Royal patronage,
and a house-building boom was in full swing. The most desirable
corner was Upper Norwood around Cintra Park, Spring Grove
and Anerley Grove. In Anerley Grove in 1841 William Hawes,
a wine merchant, lived with his family of six, plus a retinue of
five servants and servants' dependants. At Cintra Lodge Gabriel
Shaw, another merchant, presided over a household of 12: five
members of the family, and seven servants. People like Hawes
and Shaw prompted an 1844 commentator to describe Penge as

sporting '...a number of opulent residents (with) elegant mansions...'.

Growth continued through the 1840s. New homes were built along Westow Hill, down Anerley Road, and on Penge High Street and Beckenham Road, but the Upper Norwood area continued to be the most important focus for development, with Belvedere Road and Hamlet Road taking shape during the decade. Overall the housing stock increased by about 70 per cent, while the population in the same period grew by over 400 per cent, to more than 1,000. To our twenty-first-century minds, this immediately suggests over-crowding. But in fact the statistics tell a very different story – or rather they tell two different stories, one of which concerns Penge's very richest residents, and the other of which concerns its very poorest.

Firstly, as we have seen, Penge was becoming a prestigious suburb favoured by successful merchants, bankers and civil servants. These men lived in large houses, with large families, and large retinues of live-in domestic servants. So in these cases the high ratio of residents to houses, far from indicating over-crowding, signals upper-middle-class prosperity.

At the other end of the social scale a quite different factor was at work. During the 1840s Penge became home to the North Surrey District School. Built on Anerley Road in 1847 by the Poor Law Unions of Lewisham, Wandsworth and Reigate, the School's purpose was to teach 'useful trades' to poor children who had fallen into the care of their respective parishes. It was a sort of childrens' workhouse. It was also the largest single residential institution in the area: in the 1851 Census, 40 per cent of Penge's entire population was accounted for by the inmates and staff of the North Surrey School.

Penge had also become a target for one of the 'freehold societies'. These had been called into existence by the 1832 Reform Act which gave the vote to property-owners. Freehold societies were an early form of building society, driven by a self-consciously populist and radical political agenda. Their aim was to help the artisans and clerks of the lower middle class to acquire their own property, as a means of qualifying for the right to vote. During the 1840s one of these societies, the National Freehold Society, became active in Penge, buying up land on behalf of its members and thus helping the area to acquire a new lower-middle-class population.

And to complete the picture, down around Penge Green, the hamlet's original inhabitants, a small cluster of poor families working on local farms or surviving off smallholdings, were still there. The 1841 census describes one male resident after another – Boldon, Jeffery, Ansel, Croucher, Parker – simply as 'Labourer', or 'Agricultural Labourer'. Alongside them lived the occasional small farmer, craftsman, and – intriguingly – a number of policemen including James Gunnell, Zephaniah Taylor and William Shorter. Even ten years later, after a decade of constant building and development, and with Penge well-established as a desirable residential suburb with good connections to the City, this essentially rural fragment of its population persisted.

It can be seen for instance in Croydon Road, which follows the line of an ancient way, long pre-dating the road-system initiated by the enclosure of Penge Common. It was a main route across the Common, so that as former common land started to be developed it was inevitably caught up in the process. In 1851, between the junction with Penge High Street to the north-east, and Anerley Road to the south-west, there were 33 residents living in seven households along Croydon Road. Of the heads of these seven households, three were Labourers, one was a Farmer, one a Blacksmith, one a retired shopkeeper, and one a Pauper. six of the seven households contained a married couple (average age 51) plus children (usually one or two). In the seventh household Hannah Overton the Pauper lived by herself, aged 79.

Poor Hannah Overton was obviously destitute. Most of her neighbours along Croydon Road were also poor, or at best managed to scrape a hand to mouth existence. Thomas LaRue the Blacksmith may have been an exception: Blacksmiths were often skilled and respected craftsmen. And William Rogers the Farmer was certainly not poor: his unusually detailed census entry reads:

'Farmer of 700 acres employing 9 Labourers'. Rogers may have owned Clay Farm, which seems to have straddled the crest of the hill where the Robin Hood pub used to stand and the slope running down to the south-west. His relative prosperity was also marked by the fact that he supported by far the largest family on Croydon Road, with six sons and five daughters.

Charitable good works continued in the poor part of Penge during the 1840s. The Queen Dowager Adelaide, having already donated to the Watermens Almshouses, now decided to repeat the act but this time as principal sponsor. In 1849 she opened the King William IV Naval Asylum, named after her late husband, just a few yards away from the Watermens Almshouses, to provide housing for the widows of naval officers. Again the style was mock-Tudor – the inevitable style for almshouses – but rather more correctly done than the Watermens Almshouses.

John Dudin-Brown also stepped in again to meet the community's spiritual needs. The Chapel was only ten years old, but it was already becoming too small for the growing population, so he donated another parcel of land next to the Watermens Almshouses for a church to be built. He also arranged for the Watermans & Lightermans Company to support the vicar's living, but took care to ensure that the chosen vicar would reflect his own evangelical leanings. St. John's Church opened in 1849.

Putting all this together, by the beginning of the 1850s Penge was growing fast and acquiring an increasingly socially-mixed population. It still had plenty of potential for development as a well-to-do suburb, especially in the new roads radiating out from Upper Norwood. But it also had a large number of institutionalised poor in the North Surrey School, and pensioners and genteel poor in its two almshouses. And in addition to its small, long-standing group of agricultural labourers, it was starting to acquire a new lower-middle- and working-class population.

However, Penge was part of a wider economy, and in the early 1850s the building trade in London was going through one of its periodic periods of glut and slump. Locally, in 1851 there were no houses under construction, and 12 were standing empty. The construction industry trade paper *The Builder* lamented at this time that:

> ... amidst this mass of buildings which strike the eye in almost every direction, hundreds of houses remain unoccupied. How so many private residences can find occupants is a question not easily solved.

For one little corner of South London, however, help was at hand. The arrival of the Crystal Palace would help Penge to buck the trend.

Sources

Census of Great Britain 1841. (Penge enumeration tables).

Census of Great Britain 1851. (Penge enumeration tables).

Cherry, Bridget & Pevsner, Nicolaus. 1983, *London 2: South*, Penguin, Harmondsworth.

Dudley, M.R. 1980. *The Parliamentary Enclosure Movement: Penge Hamlet, c. 1780-1860.* St. Catherine's College, Cambridge.

Inman, Eric R. & Tonkin, Nancy, 1993, *Beckenham*, Phillimore, Chichester.

Inwood, Stephen, 1998, *A History of London*, Macmillan, London.

Jones, Ruth & Rooksby, Keith. 2000. *The history of St. John's the Evangelist Parish Church, Penge.* St. John's Penge.

Porter, Roy. 1996. *London, a Social History.* Penguin, Harmondsworth.

Pullen, Doris E. 1971. *Penge*, Able Publications, Knebworth.

Scott, Mick. 1995. *Crystal Palace, Penge and Anerley.* Alan Sutton Publishing Ltd., Stroud

Sheppard, Francis, 1998. *London: A History*, Oxford University Press, Oxford.

Taylor, Bessie. 1965. *Bromley, Beckenham & Penge, Kent, since 1750.* Department of Geography, Birkbeck College, London.

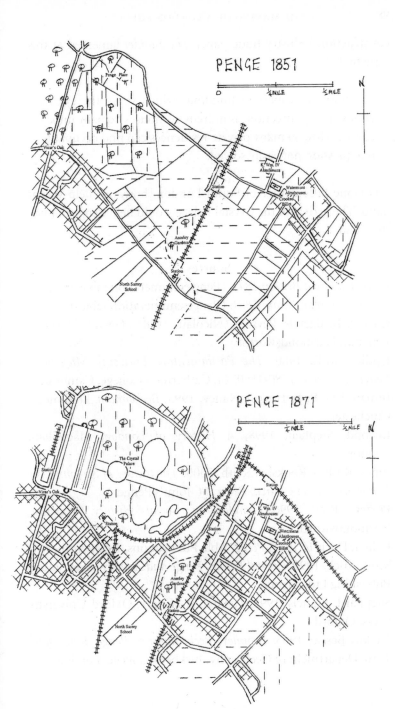

Crystal Palace site before construction

Steam engine used during construction of Crystal Palace

Navvies employed in construction of Crystal Palace

Chapter 9
'The wonderful building on the Penge Hills':
The Crystal Palace

The Great Exhibition of 1851 made Joseph Paxton into a national hero, and he made good use of this celebrity status to win the backing of the LBSCR for the re-location of the Crystal Palace to Penge. But the new Crystal Palace was far from being a mere reconstruction of the original: it was vastly bigger, with twice the area of glass, and one-and-a-half times the capacity. The original, relatively simple design was replaced by a more baroque conception. And even this expanded and elaborated building was only half the story. Overall, whereas the Hyde Park Palace had cost about £150,000, Paxton's budget for the new Penge Palace ran to £500,000.

Below the Palace itself, terraces, avenues and gardens cascaded down the hillside, together with 12,000 fountain jets, waterfalls, canals and lakes. The vision was heroic, but its realisation posed a nightmare challenge in hydraulic engineering. Paxton's original design simply failed to work – at enormous cost – and Isambard Kingdom Brunel had to be called in to save the day. Brunel's solution was to build two brick water towers at either end of the main building. In terms of building material, shape, height and location, the towers completely ruined the intended visual impact of the new Palace: John Ruskin described the final effect as resembling 'A cucumber frame between two chimneys'. But ironically the towers also became one of the Palace's most striking visual features, and even today they are clearly visible in the logo of Crystal Palace Football Club.

The Crystal Palace took two years to build, from 1852 to 1854. The great railway boom of the mid-1840s had burned itself out by this time, giving way to a period of general economic gloom. The great Crystal Palace building project was therefore a godsend for those lucky enough to work on it. And given the project's close link with the railways in general, and the LBSCR in particular, it should not surprise us to find that these lucky individuals were former railway navvies.

Navvies made up a unique and fearsome fraction of the nineteenth century working class. As we have seen, the nature of their work meant that they moved across the landscape in large gangs, roughly marshalled by railway companies and sub-contractors. Some of them had family homes far away, but many had none, and while they were on the job they tended to live in temporary shanty-towns. They were notorious for their indifference to religion, their indifference to conventional morality on matters such as marriage, and their dedication to alcohol – actively encouraged by their own bosses as a means of control. Their paganism was so well known that they attracted their very own missionaries, including a number of stalwart middle-class women who combined lectures in Christian piety with practical counselling and social work.

About 6,400 navvies worked on the Penge Palace at its peak and by the time it was finished they had written themselves into folklore as a particularly celebrated gang. They were of course used to dangerous work – on the railways, death was so common that contractors didn't even bother to keep records of the men killed. Building the Crystal Palace was safer than building a railway, though even here lives were lost, such as the 12 men killed in a single incident in August 1853 when scaffolding collapsed.

However, unlike a railway line, the Crystal Palace didn't move. If they had been building a line across a bleak Pennine moor, the navvies would simply have thrown up a series of shanty towns. But now they were in the heart of suburban South London, a few hundred yards from the highly respectable and very nervous residents of Upper Norwood. Somehow or other they had to be housed during the two years that it took to put the Palace up.

They seem to have gravitated, or been allocated, to two places. Firstly a whole new estate, Norwood New Town, was built on Central Hill specifically for the navvies and their families. It quickly acquired a reputation for drunkenness and fighting leading to complaints from Upper Norwood's residents. The authorities responded by throwing up a wall to separate the two areas, and by laying on extra police patrols at weekends, so that Norwood New Town started to take on the character of a guarded compound.

In addition, a second group set itself up down the hill in Penge, in and around Arpley Road. They also seem to have taken their lawless ways with them, and for many years this part of Penge had a particularly bad reputation. Forty years later in the 1890s, Charles Booth reported that while most of Penge's working class were 'respectable working men' there were 'rough poor' in the Arpley Road area:

> ... a relic, it is said, of the building of the Crystal Palace – that
> is of a settlement of labourers formed there at that time.

Many must have wondered what would happen when the Palace was built and the work ran out: would all the navvies stay on, unemployed and increasingly destitute? In the event, the problem was solved by the timely advent of the Crimean War, which came along just as the Crystal Palace was nearing completion. Many of the workers were quickly drafted and shipped off to Russia to dig trenches, and we may imagine that Upper Norwood breathed a sigh of relief as they watched their unwelcome neighbours depart. From the navvies' point of view, the Crimea added yet another chapter to their collective sense of history and identity: even twenty years later, workers on the Settle to Carlisle line in Cumbria still commemorated their years in the trenches by giving their shanties names such as 'Sevastopol'.

As a business proposition the Crystal Palace was blighted from the start by Paxton's extravagant design. Its original budget of £500,000 had ballooned to £1,350,000, a huge sum, by the time it opened its gates to the public in 1854. This left it with a finan-

cial hangover which never went away, and which led to ridicu-
lous and counter-productive episodes of cost-cutting: when a fire
broke out in the north transept in December 1866, it could not
be repaired or rebuilt because the Company had failed to pay the
insurance premium in order to save money.

These financial difficulties were well known and publicly
debated, rather in the way that the difficulties of the Millennium
Dome have been debated in our own day. Like the Dome, the
Crystal Palace was ultimately a commercial failure. But unlike the
Dome, and despite being plagued by these problems, the Palace
somehow held its own as a going concern and remained open
for decades, establishing itself firmly as London's greatest popular entertainment attraction. It put on concerts and a regular
Handel Festival from the 1850s, annual Firework Displays from
the 1860s, one of the first 'Zoetrope' moving-picture exhibitions
in 1868, balloon ascents, circuses, high-wire acts, and so on. For
nearly 20 years from 1895 it hosted the F.A. Cup Final. From the
mid-1850s to the mid-1880s, it attracted an average of two million visitors every year, nearly 40,000 every week. It was a massive undertaking, and it employed hundreds of workers on site,
as well as supporting thousands of jobs right across London.

People loved the Crystal Palace. Sixteen years after it first opened
its gates the *Graphic* magazine celebrated it as '...the wonderful
glass and iron building on the Penge Hills...' and dismissed its
financial problems by asserting:

> There are some places that take hold of the public sympathy
> and the public affection, and the Crystal Palace is one of
> them. We have made it our own, whatever the shareholders
> may say....

It is beyond our scope here to trace the later history of the
Crystal Palace: its nationalisation in the early twentieth century;
its service in the First World War as a Royal Navy training school;
its role in John Logie Baird's experiments in television; its final

destruction by fire in 1936. But there is an element of ironic continuity which is worth noting.

The site where the Crystal Palace and its gardens once stood is today Crystal Palace Park and the National Sports Centre. The boundaries of the Park are pretty much the same as the boundaries of the grounds of the Crystal Palace, which in turn were pretty much the same as the boundaries of the grounds of Penge Place when it was owned by Leo Schuster, and before him by John Barwell Cator, John Scott and John Morgan. Now, as we saw in Chapter 5, at some point in the 1780s John Morgan seems to have added to his land by unilaterally annexing some acres of Common. The Battersea Vestry certainly believed that he had done this, and there is no evidence that the land was ever recovered, so we must assume that Morgan successfully consolidated it into the grounds of Penge Place. It was then passed on to Scott and successive owners until it became part of the Crystal Palace, and now of the Park. The upshot is that today Crystal Palace Park probably contains the only remaining fragment of Penge Common which is still green, undeveloped, and open to the public – and this is a direct legacy of John Morgan's seizure of that land over 200 years ago precisely in order to deny it to the public.

Sources

Anthony, John. 1973. *Joseph Paxton*. Shire Publications Ltd., Princes Risborough.

Beaver, Patrick. 1986. *The Crystal Palace*, Phillimore & Co. Ltd., Chichester.

Booth, Charles. 1902. *Life and Labour of the People in London*. Third series: Religious influences: volume 6. Macmillan, London.

Coleman, Terry. 1968. *The Railway Navvies*. Penguin, Harmondsworth

Croydon Natural History & Scientific Society (CNHSS), 1979. *Victorian Croydon Illustrated*, CNHSS Ltd., Croydon.

Graphic, The. 1870. London.

Jackson, Alan. 1999. *London's Local Railways.* Capital Transport Publishing, Harrow Weald.

Pullen, Doris E. 1971. *Penge,* Able Publications, Knebworth.

Reed, Nicholas. 1995. *Camille Pissarro at Crystal Palace.* Lilburne Press, London.

Reeves, Graham. 1986. *Palace of the People.* Bromley Library Service, Bromley.

Scott, Mick. 1995. *Crystal Palace, Penge and Anerley.* Alan Sutton Publishing Ltd., Stroud

Taylor, Bessie. 1965. *Bromley, Beckenham & Penge, Kent, since 1750.* Department of Geography, Birkbeck College, London.

Chapter 10
'A waste of modern tenements': life in Penge in the late nineteenth century

With the Crystal Palace built and open for business, Penge's growth continued relentlessly. Every year of the 1850s saw net growth of 400 inhabitants, every year of the 1860s saw net growth of 800, and so it went on.

Significantly however, the number of houses was growing even more rapidly than the number of people, reversing the trend of the 1840s. This reflected a shift in the class structure of the growing population. Large houses for prosperous families with retinues of servants were still being built: sites close to the Crystal Palace and well up the hill, in Upper Norwood and along Sydenham Hill and Crystal Palace Park Road, were regarded as highly desirable. But further down, on ground which twenty-five years before had been common land, a dense mass of new housing was arising.

In the 1850s Anerley Park, Oakfield Road, Woodbine Grove and Maple Road were laid out, and in the 1860s this framework was filled in by new roads such as Thicket Road, and by side-roads such as Castledine Road off Anerley Park; Cambridge Grove, Laurel Grove, and Malcolm Road off Oakfield Road; and Jasmine Grove, Hawthorn Grove, and Heath Grove off Maple Road. Meanwhile to the north-east of the High Street, Crampton Road, Station Road, Forbes (now called Mosslea) Road, Queen Adelaide Road, and Wordsworth Road appeared. These streets, further down the hill and closer to the traditional heart of the hamlet at Penge Green, had a more complex social character than the prosperous avenues higher up. They included villas for prosperous households with servants, but they also contained a growing number of smaller terraced houses and cottages for working-class and lower-middle-class families.

Penge was no longer pretty. Where once there had been open land, woodland and rough grass, now there was a carpet of roads and houses. The only reminder of Penge Common's existence lay in street names which recalled some of its trees and plants – Oakfield Road, Maple Road, Thicket Road, Hawthorn Grove, and so on. By the 1870s one visitor went so far as to describe Penge as '… a waste of modern tenements, mean, monotonous and wearisome…'.

A tantalising flavour of life in Penge in the late 19th Century can be captured from Charles Booth's monumental study of 'The Life and Labour of the People in London'. This was conducted over several years in the 1890s, and is peppered with terms of description which to our ears indicate casual class prejudice. Thus his 'Class A' consists of 'occasional labourers, loafers, semi-criminals', and he was perfectly happy to condemn certain streets or neighbourhoods as 'being of bad character'. But despite this – perhaps partly because of it – his surveys make fascinating and lively reading. And they are based on a careful statistical analysis by which he quantified and compared the extent of poverty of late nineteenth century London.

Booth combined Penge with Sydenham as a single statistical district, but these two areas were pretty similar in class and social terms and this need not bother us too much. He found that 40 per cent of the population was made up of the regularly-employed working class whom he described as 'respectable working men', although of course the figure also included women and children. Another 40 per cent consisted of the 'lower middle class and above'. The remaining 20 per cent lived in poverty, though even here most were not outright paupers or 'loafers' but were getting by in a hand-to-mouth way through occasional casual work. This 20 per cent poverty rating was the lowest figure recorded by Booth anywhere in South London, for which the overall average was 31 per cent, with the worst destitution found in Southwark (68 per cent) and Greenwich (65 per cent).

Penge in the late nineteenth century had clearly come a long way from the exclusive upper-middle-class suburb of the 1840s and 1850s. The area had changed in its class character and culture. But these changes were not the result of some external force violating Penge's quiet respectability from without. On the contrary, they derived directly from the area's earlier phase as a select upper-middle-class suburb, allied to the formidable presence of the Crystal Palace as a powerful local economic motor.

We saw in Chapter 3 that the nineteenth century middle-class way of life was very labour intensive. For reasons of status, respectability, and practicality, upper-middle-class families employed whole teams of servants lodged permanently in their houses, and in addition they engaged small armies of tradesmen, craftsmen and suppliers on a daily basis. Further down the social scale, lower-middle-class families too felt the need for a modest level of domestic service, even if it was only a single house-maid who came in each day from her own home. All of this created a considerable demand for labour, but in the absence of cheap public transport the providers of this labour had necessarily to live in or close to the middle-class households that provided them with a livelihood. 'Exclusive' middle-class suburbs therefore tended over time to call into existence their own local working-class populations, with their own identities, needs and desires, and thus undermined the very 'exclusivity' which they set out to protect.

This social dynamic was rooted in its own particular time and place. It was certainly not an expression of some universal law of suburban expansion: in our own time, the advent of the private car has transformed the meaning and politics of suburban growth. But in nineteenth-century London the social processes at work were very different, reflecting in particular the presence of mass labour-intensive personal services coupled with the absence of mass easily-accessible public transport. And in the particular case of Penge, working-class growth was driven not only by middle-class demand for domestic and other personal services, but also by the great job-creation machine just up the hill at the Crystal Palace.

By the 1890s, therefore, Penge was no longer posh, but it still craved respectability. One measure of this respectability was in bread-winning: male heads of household, both working class and lower middle class, were expected to hold down regular jobs and bring in a regular income for their families – and Booth's study shows that by and large, in Penge and Sydenham, most of them did.

Another measure of respectability was found in attitudes to religion – or, to be more accurate, attitudes to religious institutions. Lack of piety in working-class neighbourhoods was a major cause for concern among society's self-appointed moral guardians in the later nineteenth century. South London and East London in particular were notorious for having the lowest church attendances in the country. Booth reports that Sunday was seen as a day for lying in, a big dinner, the pub and general recreation. Going to church was not the priority:

> The general attitude of the working class towards religion is … indifference, and they are said to be infected with the spirit of London as summed up in the phrase "We know what we want and we shall do what we like".

This indifference provoked a wave of middle-class church-building and evangelism. Penge Chapel was built in the early 1840s, and was quickly followed by St. John's Church in 1849. By the 1890s there was a number of other churches and chapels in the area. Holy Trinity Church on Lennard Road had been built in the 1870s, sponsored by tea merchant Francis Peek (of Peek Frean), Albermarle Cator who donated the land, and Anne Dudin-Brown who continued her family's philanthropic tradition with financial support. In addition, there were Congregationalist and Wesleyan chapels. Booth reports attendances at St. John's as large and enthusiastic but consisting of 'exclusively middle and upper-class people', and at the non-conformist chapels too congregations were 'well to do'.

Penge's working class therefore seems to have been gripped by the same laxity regarding religious observance as workers elsewhere in London. But indifference to Sunday observance did not mean indifference to the church as a social institution. Booth found that despite the 'exclusively middle and upper class' character of St. John's congregation, its day-school was well-attended by local working-class children. But, he went on, this had nothing to do with religion. It was due 'solely to (the church school) being considered more respectable'. Even if local working-class families did not feel the need actually to attend church on Sundays, they still saw the church as an institution steeped in social status and propriety and esteem, and they were quite happy to have some of it rub off on their children.

In addition to worrying about working-class indifference to religion, middle-class moral guardians also found grounds for concern on the question of drink. In the 1860s Penge had a reputation as a drinkers' paradise. It had 22 public houses, 16 of them nestling cheek by jowl along the 700 yards of High Street between Oakfield Road and Croydon Road. Significantly, this was just a few yards down the road from the Penge Entrance to the Crystal Palace, which suggests that a major element of the demand for alcohol came not from local residents, but from visitors to the Palace finishing off their big day out with a pint or two before heading home.

However, popular attitudes towards alcohol seemed to shift over the 30 years from the 1860s to the 1890s. In the 1860s, pubs were mainly male refuges, and rowdy drunkenness was common. By the 1890s, it was increasingly common for women to visit pubs, either with male partners or in groups of female friends. According to Booth this was widely seen as moderating the behaviour of men: overt rowdy drunkenness was now seen as offensive and unmanly. In fact some complained that women were more likely than men to drink to excess.

Finally, the explosion in Penge's population in the 1860s brought an actual or perceived increase in crime. Although policemen are recorded as having lived in the area as early as the 1840s, they had no official base. So in 1870 the Parish Council petitioned for a local Police Station to be built, citing '…an increase in crime (due to) the growth of poverty and want of employment of the lower classes of the locality'.

The station was built on the High Street, more or less opposite Arpley Road, which as we have seen was widely regarded as a street of bad character. Arpley Road is long gone, but the police station is still there, and is now the oldest continuously surviving Metropolitan Police Station in London.

In Chapter 8 we took a snapshot of life along Croydon Road at the beginning of the 1850s. If we leap forward 20 years to the early 1870s, we will find many of the themes of this chapter – population growth, changing class structure, the explosion in female employment as domestic servants – illustrated in detail.

In 1851, between the junction with the High Street at the bottom and the junction with Anerley Road at the top, there were seven households containing 33 inhabitants, most of whom were of modest means or working poor. The one exception was a prosperous farmer. By 1871, the number of households and inhabitants had increased eightfold: 268 people living in 55 households. They were a complex social mix, but with the same rough class geography hinted at in 1851 – poorer at the bottom of the road, wealthier further up.

Starting near the bottom, at no. 7, the Lee and Castle families kept down costs by sharing a house. The Lees were in their 40s, and the Castles in their 20s. Both couples were unusual in not having any children – or at least none with them to be recorded on census day – because most working-class families along the road had one or two children. No occupation is recorded for either of the two wives, but both men were Gardeners, which was the single most common job reported for working-class men living in Croydon Road. This is a classic example of a local service occupation, utterly dependent on the close proximity of wealthy upper-middle-class households with large gardens. Most of these gardeners would have scraped by on a casual basis, doing odd seasonal jobs for various wealthy households in the area, or perhaps in the ornamental gardens of the Crystal Palace itself. A possible exception was Hezekiah Faulkner who lived at no. 9 and is described as a 'Head Gardener'. As such, he may have had a more secure position at the Crystal Palace or over-seeing the upkeep of one or more private gardens in the area.

Like most of their neighbours these families had come to Penge from elsewhere in their search for work. The Lees came from Ireland, as did Mrs. Castle. Her husband had been born in Gloucestershire, and Hezekiah Faulkner in Berkshire. Among their neighbours the single most common place of birth was Suffolk. Only three adult residents of Croydon Road in 1871 had been born within five miles of Penge. This was a growing, churning community, a place of immigrants and new arrivals.

Moving up the road, and up the social scale, at No. 7 Goldsmiths Terrace we find Mr. and Mrs. Stanley with their four children. Stanley was a maths teacher, presumably either working in a local school or giving private instruction. He was in his mid 30s, and both he and his wife had moved down to Penge from London: he came from Islington and she from Shoreditch. They did not have any live-in servants but as a teacher, needing to maintain a certain standing in the community, we might expect Stanley to have engaged a domestic servant on a daily basis to clean, cook and generally keep up appearances.

Finally, running up Croydon Road on the south-east side, clearly visible on the 1871 Ordnance Survey map, was a series of large detached houses with extensive gardens. Prosperous upper-middle-class families lived here:- in Elm View we find William Matthews, an umbrella manufacturer, with his wife, daughter, and two servants; in Headley Lodge, John Fleet, a 'Colonial Dealer', with wife, four children, two boarders, and two servants; in Clifton Lodge, John Creswell, a surgeon, with wife, five children, sister in law, visitor, boarder, and five servants; and so on. Like their poorer neighbours down the road, these people too had come to Penge from other parts of the country. Presumably the heads of household saw it as a convenient and sufficiently-fashionable place to provide safe lodging for their families while they pursued their business affairs in and around London. The most commonly-reported birthplaces for these respectable businessmen and professionals were the west country, especially Devon or Somerset; London (i.e. the cities of London and Westminster); and Middlesex (i.e. much of what is now North and West London).

The single most common occupation among residents of Croydon Road in 1871 was that of domestic servant. This was part of a wider pattern: the second half of the nineteenth century saw an explosion in the numbers employed in domestic service in London, up by 40 per cent between 1851 and 1891. Along Croydon Road there were 50 servants, overwhelmingly young women with an average age of 23. Again they had come to Penge from elsewhere, though not from as far afield as the working-class residents at the bottom of the road, or their own upper-middle-class employers nearer the top. Most of them came from London, Middlesex, Kent (which in 1871 included such places as Greenwich and Deptford) or elsewhere in Surrey (which included Kennington, Southwark, and Penge itself).

As part of his survey of London life and labour, Booth looked closely at this large segment of the labour force. He reported that a well-to-do household was normally 'complete in all its functions' so long as it had three servants: cook, parlour-maid and housemaid. Of these, the cook was the senior figure, the most skilled, and the most likely to make a career of it. Thus the oldest of all the domestic servants along Croydon Road was a cook aged 46. Most parlour-maids and housemaids, however, had no intention of making a career of it. They were young working-class women, earning a living for themselves for a few years for a bit of independence, or because their parents gave them no choice. Some must have regarded it as preferable to factory-work or shop-work, and may have felt that daily proximity to wealthy and respectable employers held out the promise of social advancement. But essentially the work was dull and monotonous, and life was sometimes very lonely, especially in 'single-hand' households where one young woman was expected to do all the work and spend most of her waking hours on duty. Booth reports that girls from workhouse schools – such as the North Surrey School in Anerley – were generally preferred over those who came from their own family homes. It speaks volumes that the best qualification for domestic service was an orphan childhood of institutionalisation, discipline and punishment.

Sources

Booth, Charles. 1902. *Life and Labour of the People in London.* Third series: Religious influences: volume 6. Macmillan, London.

Booth, Charles. 1902. *Life and Labour of the People in London.* Final volume. Macmillan, London.

Booth, Charles. 1904. *Life and Labour of the People in London.* First series: Poverty: volume 2. Macmillan, London

Census of Great Britain 1851. (Penge enumeration tables).

Census of Great Britain 1871. (Penge enumeration tables).

Cherry, Bridget & Pevsner, Nicolaus. 1983. *London 2: South.* Penguin, Harmondsworth.

Dudley, M.R. 1980. *The Parliamentary Enclosure Movement: Penge Hamlet, c. 1780-1860.* St. Catherine's College, Cambridge.

Inman, Eric R. & Tonkin, Nancy. 1993, *Beckenham,* Phillimore, Chichester.

Inwood, Stephen. 1998. *A History of London,* Macmillan, London.

Porter, Roy. 1996. *London, a Social History.* Penguin, Harmondsworth.

Pullen, Doris E. 1971. *Penge,* Able Publications, Knebworth.

Scott, Mick. 1995. *Crystal Palace, Penge and Anerley.* Alan Sutton Publishing Ltd., Stroud

Searle, Muriel V. 1989. *Beckenham and Penge in old picture postcards,* European Library – Zaltbommel/Netherlands.

Sheppard, Francis. 1998. *London: A History,* Oxford University

Press, Oxford.

Taylor, Bessie. 1965. *Bromley, Beckenham & Penge, Kent, since 1750*. Department of Geography, Birkbeck College, London.

Thorne, J. 1876. *Handbook to the Environs of London*, vol. 2. John Murray, London.

Chapter 11
Conclusions

This little book has tried to unpick the landscape of one small corner of suburban London; to look beyond the over-familiar sights which present themselves to our eyes – roads, railways, houses – in order to discover why they take these particular forms. Why does this railway line run along this particular route? Why are there rows of small terraced houses down here, and avenues of large detached houses up there? Why has this land over here been built upon, while that land over there is a park?

Of course, there is a particular, contingent answer to each of these particular questions. But underlying them all is a single bigger question: Why is this place – Penge – as it is? And to that there is a single big answer: Because it is a suburb of a great capitalist city, formed at a particular moment in that city's development. The physical layout of Penge today is a form of historical document. The circumstances of its formation, the pressures and priorities of nineteenth century urban capitalism, are inscribed in today's suburban landscape.

Within this framework, let us review and summarise the essential points that have emerged.

From the sixteenth to the early twentieth centuries, London was a unique urban phenomenon. It was unprecedented in terms of physical size, population density, and volume of economic activity; and in terms of the brutal effectiveness with which it performed its twin roles of national capital and global metropolis. In this little book we can hardly touch upon London's extraordinary story. But even so, we have established that the relationship between the urban centre and the suburbs was crucial to its expansion. From the seventeenth century certain inner suburbs acted as unlicensed zones of unregulated production and circulation, championing raw market forces of supply and demand against the mediated social market of the guilds. At the same time, further out, new suburban settlements were defining themselves as prestigious semi-rural retreats for the prosperous middle class, Clapham being a classic example.

However, south of the river, a general opening up of new suburbs was only possible once reliable access across the Thames had been established. For a long time, the only fixed crossing was at London Bridge. In order to build more bridges, property developers took on and defeated traditional groups such as the Watermens and Lightermens Guild. New road bridges appeared from the early eighteenth century, followed by new residential commuter suburbs south of the river. At first commuters travelled to work by foot, horse-back or coach. But the construction of London Bridge railway station in the 1830s opened up the possibility of commuting by rail: it was Penge's rail link to London Bridge which enabled its own transformation from hamlet into suburb.

The construction of new road bridges across the Thames, as a precondition for extensive and profitable property development, provides a fine example of the production of capitalist space: the production of a physical environment organised for commodity production, circulation and consumption. In Penge itself the enclosure of the Common was the vital first step in this process, transforming hundreds of acres of communally-shared land into a patchwork of privately-owned properties. This was followed by successive infrastructural projects which, one by one, reorganised the local landscape around the priorities of capital: the Croydon Canal, the London to Croydon Railway, Anerley Gardens, and finally the combined package of the Crystal Palace together with a network of new railway lines to serve it. And at the same time, thousands upon thousands of new houses went up as the suburb coalesced around these major developments: firstly substantial houses for prosperous middle-class families in Upper Norwood; then a mixture of large detached, comfortable semi-detached, and small terraced houses spreading down and across the hillside where Penge Common used to be.

Each of these various undertakings, from the vast ambition of the Crystal Palace down to little groups of houses thrown up by jobbing builders in the heart of Penge, represented a speculative investment undertaken in the hope of realising a profit. For capital, time is money: turnover time, the speed at which a commodity can be produced, brought to market, and sold, is the key to profitability and ultimately survival. Cities act as nurseries of capital because the volume and intensity of their economic activity, packed into a relatively compressed physical space, hold out the prospect of reduced turnover time. In Penge, this principle is seen most clearly in the case of the failed Croydon Canal. Its failure stemmed precisely from its inability to deliver sufficient quantities of goods to market sufficiently quickly.

The Canal also shows up the inherent tension within capitalist urban infrastructure between its character as an investment intended to generate profit, and its character as a use-value performing a practical function in the world. The Canal as a business was a commercial disaster, but the Canal as a piece of engineering was a triumph, a rich resource of fixed social capital which underpinned the subsequent construction of South London's first railway, and thus the emergence of South London's first railway suburbs.

Like many other new suburbs in the nineteenth century, Penge projected itself in its early years as a prestigious, exclusive, semi-rural retreat for the prosperous upper middle class. It promised an elegant and leisured family life among genteel middle-class neighbours, physically distant from the city's crowds, stink, noise and hazards. At the same time it promised to the male head of the household easy access to that same city as a source of employment and wealth.

But this suburban promise was intrinsically undeliverable, containing within itself the conditions of its own denial. The middle-class lifestyle was predicated upon the constant physical proximity of a host of personal and domestic servants, tradesmen, craftsmen and suppliers, all of whom – given the available forms of transport – had to live nearby. Precisely by trying to remain narrowly middle class, many suburbs ended up achieving the exact opposite, and became increasingly socially complex. We saw this happen in Penge by studying the residents of Croydon Road between 1851 and 1871. Between those two dates, the road acquired a significant number of large detached houses inhabited by prosperous middle-class families. But at the same time, and as a direct consequence, it also acquired a whole new working-class population. By 1871, the single most common occupation on Croydon Road was that of domestic servant.

Penge is an unpretentious, unremarkable, resolutely unfashionable London railway suburb. It is an ordinary little place. But to be ordinary is not to be uninteresting, or unimportant. In order to understand the transformation of Penge's landscape, we have been forced to consider much larger issues such as the nature of London, the nature of capitalist cities, and the nature of capital itself. Our sub-title, 'Capital Comes to Penge', may be a bit of a joke, but like all the best jokes, at its heart it is deadly serious. Capital did in fact come to Penge, and it made Penge the place that it is today.

Bibliography

Anthony, John. 1973. *Joseph Paxton*. Shire Publications Ltd., Princes Risborough.

Bailey, Paul. 1996. *The Oxford Book of London*, Oxford University Press, Oxford.

Battersea Vestry, Minutes of Proceedings, held in Battersea Library, Local History Department, Lavender Hill, London.

Beaver, Patrick. 1986. *The Crystal Palace*, Phillimore & Co. Ltd., Chichester.

Booth, Charles. 1902. *Life and Labour of the People in London*. Third series: Religious influences: volume 6. Macmillan, London.

Booth, Charles. 1902. *Life and Labour of the People in London*. Final volume. Macmillan, London.

Booth, Charles. 1904. *Life and Labour of the People in London*. First series: Poverty: volume 2. Macmillan, London

Brooke, Christopher, 1967. *The Saxon and Norman Kings*. Fontana, London.

Census of Great Britain 1841. (Penge enumeration tables).

Census of Great Britain 1851. (Penge enumeration tables).

Census of Great Britain 1861. (Penge enumeration tables).

Census of Great Britain 1871. (Penge enumeration tables).

Cherry, Bridget & Pevsner, Nicolaus. 1983. *London 2: South*. Penguin, Harmondsworth.

Cobbett, William, 1967. *Rural Rides*. Penguin, Harmondsworth.

Corbett Anderson, D., 1889. *Croydon Inclosure*. Private publication, Croydon.

Croydon Natural History & Scientific Society (CNHSS), 1979. *Victorian Croydon Illustrated*, CNHSS Ltd., Croydon.

Cobbett, William, 1967. *Rural Rides*, Penguin, Harmondsworth.

Coleman, Terry. 1968. *The Railway Navvies*. Penguin, Harmondsworth

Cowie, Robert with Harding, Charlotte. 2000. 'Saxon settlement and economy from the Dark Ages to Domesday' in *The Archaeology of Greater London*, Museum of London, London.

Dickens, Charles. 1998. 'Dombey and Son' in *Victorian Masterworks*, Magic Mouse Multimedia (CD-ROM).

Dudley, M.R. 1980. *The Parliamentary Enclosure Movement: Penge Hamlet, c. 1780-1860.* St. Catherine's College, Cambridge.

Filmer, J.L., 'The Norman Family of Bromley Common', in *Bromley Local History*, no. 2, 1977. Local History Society for the London Borough of Bromley.

Fowler H.W. and Fowler F.G. (eds.). 1964. *The Concise Oxford Dictionary of Current English.* Oxford University Press, Oxford.

Friends of the Great North Wood. 1986. *The Great North Wood.* London.

Friends of the Great North Wood. 1995. *From the Nun's Head to the Screaming Alice.* London.

Gilbert, Bob. 1991. *The Green London Way.* Lawrence & Wishart, London.

Graphic, The. 1870. London

Harvey, David, 2001(a). 'The geography of capitalist accumulation' in *Spaces of Capital*, Edinburgh University Press.

Harvey, David, 2001(b). 'The geopolitics of capitalism' in *Spaces of Capital*, Edinburgh University Press.

Harwood, Elain & Saint, Andrew. 1991. *London.* HMSO, London.

Hasted, E., 1983. *The History & Topography of Kent: Pt. 111, Beckenham, Bromley*, reprinted from 2nd edition of 1797, P.M.E. Erwood, Sidcup.

Hobsbawm, E.J. 1968. *Industry and Empire*, Weidenfeld & Nicholson, London.

Inwood, Stephen. 1998. *A History of London*, Macmillan, London.

Inman, Eric R. & Tonkin, Nancy. 1993. *Beckenham*, Phillimore, Chichester.

Jackson, Alan. 1999. *London's Local Railways.* Capital Transport Publishing, Harrow Weald.

Jones, Edward & Woodward, Christopher. 1992. *A Guide to the Architecture of London.* Weidenfeld & Nicholson, London.

Jones, Ruth & Rooksby, Keith. 2000. *The history of St. John's the*

Evangelist Parish Church, Penge. St. John's, Penge.

Knowlden, Patricia. 1977. 'Village into Suburb' in *Bromley Local History*, no. 2. Local History Society for the London Borough of Bromley.

Lefebvre, Henri. 1973. *The Survival of Capitalism*, Allison & Busby, London.

Lefebvre, Henri. 1991. *The Production of Space*, Basil Blackwell, Oxford.

Linebaugh, Peter. 1993. *The London Hanged*, Penguin, Harmondsworth.

Living History Publications. 1986. *Retracing Canals from Croydon to Camberwell*, Living History Publications, East Grinstead.

Mabey, Richard. 1998. *Flora Britannica* (concise edition). Chatto & Windus, London.

Marx, Karl, 1954. *Capital: A Critique of Political Economy (volume 1)*, Lawrence & Wishart, London.

Marx, Karl, 1973. *Grundrisse*, Penguin, Harmondsworth.

Marx, Karl. 1979. 'Letter to Danielson, 10/4/1879' reprinted in De La Haye, Yves (ed.), 1979, *Marx and Engels on the Means of Communication*, International General, New York.

Marx, Karl & Engels, Frederick, 1968. 'Manifesto of the Communist Party' in *Karl Marx and Frederick Engels: Selected Works in One Volume*, Lawrence & Wishart, London.

Miele, Chris. 1999. 'From aristocratic ideal to middle class idyll: 1690-1840' in *London Suburbs,* Saint, Andrew (intro.), Merrell Holberton, London.

Moffatt, Alistair. 1999. *Arthur and the Lost Kingdoms,* Weidenfeld & Nicholson, London.

Morris, John. 1973. *The Age of Arthur.* Weidenfeld & Nicholson, London.

Mumford, Lewis. 1940. *The Culture of Cities,* Secker & Warburg, London.

Mumford, Lewis. 1961. *The City in History*, Penguin, Harmondsworth.

Pearson, John. 2000. *Blood Royal.* Harper Collins, London.

Piper, Alan. 1996. *A History of Brixton.* The Brixton Society,

London.

Porter, Roy. 1996. *London, a Social History.* Penguin, Harmondsworth.

Pullen, Doris E. 1971. *Penge,* Able Publications, Knebworth.

Rackham, Oliver. 1986. *The History of the Countryside.* Phoenix Press.

Reed, Nicholas. 1995. *Camille Pissarro at Crystal Palace.* Lilburne Press, London.

Reeves, Graham. 1986. *Palace of the People.* Bromley Library Service, Bromley.

Schofield, John. 1993. *The Building of London from the Conquest to the Great Fire.* Sutton Publishing, Stroud.

Scott, Mick. 1995. *Crystal Palace, Penge and Anerley.* Alan Sutton Publishing Ltd., Stroud

Searle, Muriel V. 1989. *Beckenham and Penge in old picture postcards,* European Library; Zaltbommel/Netherlands.

Sheppard, Francis. 1998. *London: A History,* Oxford University Press, Oxford.

Taylor, Bessie. 1965. *Bromley, Beckenham & Penge, Kent, since 1750.* Department of Geography, Birkbeck College, London.

Taylor, John George. 1925. *Our Lady of Batersey.* George White, London.

Thorne, J. 1876. *Handbook to the Environs of London,* vol. 2. John Murray, London.

Thorold, Peter. 2001. *The London Rich.* Penguin, Harmondsworth.

Victoria Histories of the Counties of England: Surrey, 1967. Reprint of 1912 edition. Dawson, London.

Vine, P.A.L. 1986. *London's Lost Route to the Sea.* David & Charles, Newton Abbot.

Wandle Group, The. 1997. *The Wandle Guide,* London Borough of Sutton Leisure Services.

White, Ken. 1989. *The Croydon Canal and its Neighbours.* Ken White (privately published), London.

Index

Adams, ER 62
Addington Palace 31
Addiscombe 87
Adelaide (queen) 94, 97
Alleyn, Edward 29
Almshouses
  Watermens 55, 94, 97
  King William IV 94, 97
Anerley 41, 69, 74
  Anerley railway station 80
  Anerley Gardens 80-1, 84, 120
Ansel, Mr 96
Arpley Road 105, 114
Arun, River 71, 75
Auckland, Lord 71

Baird, John Logie 106
Barbon, Nicholas 21
Baring, Sir Francis 71
Barnard's Farm 43
Bartlett, Thomas 52
Battersea 17, 31, 33, 39-43, 48-50, 54,
  63-6
  Parish 93
  Vestry 49-61, 63-6, 74, 107
  Vicar 59, 61
Beckenham 42-3, 54-5, 57, 60, 72,
74, 86
  Parish 93
  Beckenham Place 31, 55
Beddington Place 29
Bedford, Duke of 31
Belair, 31
Bermondsey 28, 43
Blackfriars railway station 81
Blackheath 32
Boldon, Mr 96
Bolingbroke, Viscounts (St John
family) 42, 48, 55
Booth, Charles 105, 110, 112-13,
  116-7
Booth, William 62
Brixton 31-2, 39, 86,

Bromley 38, 43, 55, 74, 86
Brunel, Isambard Kingdom 103
building lease system 21-22, 34-5, 121
Burney, Fanny 55

Camberwell 30, 38, 42
'Canal Mania' 69-70
Cannon Street railway station 81
capital, capitalism ix, 2
  and cities 2-9
  and London 22-4, 119-22
  and railways 77-9
Carew family 29
Carshalton 28
Castle family 114-5
Catford 72
Cator
  Albemarle 112
  Albert 94
  Family/Cator Estate 87-8
  John 55-6, 60-1
  John Barwell 56-62, 65, 107
  Joseph 56-7
  Colonel W 94
Chaffinch, River 41
Charing Cross railway station 81
churches/religion
  Congregationalist Chapel 112
  Holy Trinity Church 112
  Penge Chapel 93-4, 97, 112
  Popular attitudes to religion 112-13
  St John's Church 97, 112-13
  Wesleyan Chapel 112
cities
  Medieval 1-2
  Capitalist 2-9
City of London 12, 16-21, 28-30, 32,
  43, 49, 84, 116
Clapham 29-30, 33-4, 87, 120
  Clapham Sect 93
Clay Farm 97
Clerkenwell 19
Clock House 41

coach services 30, 32, 43
Cobbett, William 31-2, 57-8
Coper's Cope Farm 55
Creswell family 115
Crimean War 105
Croham Hurst 38
Crooked Billet (public house) 54-5,
    61-2, 94
Croucher, Mr 96
Croydon 28, 41-2, 54, 69-70, 72-3, 75,
    79, 81, 87
Croydon Canal 43, 62, 63, 69-76, 79,
    120-1
  commercial failure 75, 93
  construction 71-3
  Croydon Canal Company 56, 58,
    73-5, 80
  owners, investors 71
  Penge 56, 74-5
  Portsmouth 71-5
  and railway 75-6
  routes 72
Croydon Road, Penge 62, 94, 96-7,
    114-6, 122
Crystal Palace 81, 84-5, 111-2, 115,
    120-1
  construction 103-4
  Crystal Palace Company 83
  Crystal Palace Football Club 103
  Crystal Palace Park 107
  Crystal Palace railway station 84
  Crystal Palace High Level railway
    station/line 85-6
  FA Cup Finals 106
  finances 103, 105-6
  fire 107
  Great Exhibition/Hyde Park 82-3,
    103
  navvies 104-5
  owners/investors 83
  parliamentary support 84-5
  and railways 82-6
  visitors 106
Cubitt, Thomas 33

Defoe, Daniel 29
Denmark Hill 31

Deptford 28, 43, 70, 72, 116
Devon 116
Dickens, Charles 77-8
Dodd, Ralph 72
domestic servants 32, 111, 116-7
Dudin-Brown, Anne 112
Dudin-Brown, John 94, 97
Dudley, Mr 64
Dulwich 29, 32, 86

Eadwig (king) 38-9
Edge, Mr 58
Edward (king: the Confessor) 39, 41
Elizabeth I (queen) 11, 41-2
Eltham 29
Enclosure 13-14, 47-48, 53
  (see also Penge: Common)
Epsom 29-30
Essex 14

Faulkner, Hezekiah 115
Fleet family 115
Forest Hill 72
Fox, William 62
Fox and Henderson 82-3
Foxgrove Farm 55
French Revolution 70

Gloucestershire 115
Grand Imperial Ship Canal 75
Graphic magazine 106
Great Exhibition See Crystal Palace
Great North Wood 37
Greenwich 29, 81, 116,
Greyhound (public house) 74
Gunnell, James 96
Gwydir, Lord 55, 71

Hammett, Sir Benjamin 71
Harold (king) 39
Harrison, John 51
Hastings, Battle of 39
Hawes, William 94
Hayes 87
Henry VIII (king) 13, 41, 42
Herne Hill 31, 86
Hertfordshire 14, 16, 39
Heydon family 29

Holborn 19
Humphreys, Mr 52, 57

Ireland 115
Islington 115

Johnson, Samuel 55

Kennington, 116
  Kennington Palace 29
Kent 14, 41, 116
Kent House Farm 55

Labour power 4
Laing, Samuel, MP 83-4
Lambeth 28, 42
Langley 38
LaRue, Thomas 96
Lawrie, John 62
Lee family 114-5
Lewisham 87
London
  and capitalism 22-4, 119-22
  employment 15-18, 23-24
  fire 20-21, 29
  immigration 12-15
  and Industrial Revolution 24
  population 11-12, 19
  mortality, plague 12
  South London 28-35, 120
  suburbs 16-22, 27, 32
London and Birmingham railway 77
London and Brighton Railway
Company 81
London and Croydon Railway
Company 75, 79-81, 87, 93, 120
London Bridge railway station 69, 76,
  79, 81, 84-5, 87, 120
London Brighton and South Coast
Railway Company 33, 81-5, 103-4
London Chatham and Dover Railway
Company 33, 85-6

Matthews family 115
Middlesex 14, 16, 116,
Mid-Kent railway line 87-8
Morgan, John 48, 50-3, 56-7, 60, 65,
  71, 107
Mortain, Robert Count of 39

Napoleon 71
navvies 78, 104-5
National Freehold Society 96
Nelson, Horatio 49, 73
New Beckenham railway station 87
New Cross 72-3
Newgate 18
Nine Elms 33
Nonsuch Palace 29
North Surrey District School 95, 97,
  117
Norwood Grove 31
Norwood Junction railway station
  74, 84,
Norwood New Town 105,

Odo (bishop) 39
Overton, Hannah 96

Parker, Mr 96
Paxton, Joseph 82, 84, 103, 105
Peckham 85-6
Peek, Francis 112
Penge
  'Beating the bounds',
  'perambulations' 42, 54, 57
  Common 47-66, 72, 74, 80, 93, 107,
  120
  crime 114
  Croydon Canal 56, 74-5
  'Detached hamlet of Battersea'
  39-40, 42-3
  Domesday Book 28, 40
  eighteenth century boundaries 54
  farms 43
  house building 80, 93-5, 97-8, 109-
  10, 120-1
  name 37-8
  National Freehold Society 96
  North Surrey District School 95,
  97, 117
  Penge Green 61, 96, 109
  Penge Place 56, 57, 74, 83, 107
  Penge East railway station 86
  Penge West railway station 74, 80
  Penge Wharf 74-5, 80
  police station 114

population 43, 109
public houses 113
seventeenth century boundaries
41-2
social class 94-7, 109-17, 121-2
woods, woodland, timber 38-41,
43, 53, 74
Pepys, Samuel 29
Peyton, Richard 61
Plaistow Lodge 31
Pool, River 72
Poor Law 50
Portsmouth 71-5,
production of space 4-7, 16-22, 120

railways
and capitalism 77-9
and Crystal Palace 82-6
navvies 78, 104-5
owners/investors 79
routes 78-9
and suburbs/commuters 33-4, 83-4,
87, 120
Ravensbourne, River 72
Rennie, John 72, 75
Reynolds, Joshua 55
Robin Hood (public house) 97
Rockhills 41
Rogers, William 96
Rotherhithe 53, 70, 72
Royal Navy 71, 106
Russell, Lord 71

Sanderson, William 62, 80-1, 84
Schuster, Leo 83-4, 107
Scott, John 53-9, 65, 71, 74, 107
Selhurst 38, 72
servants, domestic servants 32, 111,
116-7
Shaw, Gabriel 94
Shirley 38
Shoreditch 115
Shorter, William 96
Somerset 116
South Eastern Railway Company
86-7
Southwark 19, 28, 116

space, urban space, production of
4-7, 16-22, 120
Spencer
Earl George 49-50, 52, 56, 59-61,
63-4
Earl John 31, 48, 55, 59-60
Stanley family 115
Stowe, John 16, 20
Streatham 29, 39
suburbs 27-8
production of suburban space 16-
22
railways 33-4, 83-4, 87, 120
social class 32-4, 121-2
South London 28-35
Suffolk 115
Surrey 14, 16, 28, 39, 41, 116
Surrey Docks 70
Surrey Iron Railway 71, 73, 79-80
Sussex 39
Swabey, Mr 51
Swingate Farm 43
Sydenham 29, 54, 72-4, 86, 110

Taylor, Zephaniah 96
Thames, River 30-31, 39, 69, 72, 74
Thames bridges 30-31, 120
Thrale, Mrs 55
Thurlow, Lord 52
Trafalgar, Battle of 73
Tunbridge Wells 29
turnover time 7, 70-2, 121
turnpikes 69

Upper Norwood 94-5, 97, 104-5, 109,
120

Vicar's Oak 41-2
Victoria railway station 81, 85-6

Walworth 38
Wandle, River 28, 73
Wandsworth 18, 28, 73
Waterloo railway station 81, 86
Watermen and Lightermen 30-1
Watermens and Lightermens
Company 94, 97, 120
Wellington, Duke of 70

West Croydon railway station 79
Westminster 116
  Westminster Abbey 39-41
Westow Hill, Upper Norwood 95
Wey, River, 71, 75
Wickham Court 29
William (king: the Conqueror) 39-40
Willmore, River 41
Wilson, Mr 51
Wilson, William 62